Motorbooks International

FARM TRACTOR COLOR HISTORY

FARM CRAWLERS

Text by Robert N. Pripps

Photography by Andrew Morland

For Uncle Norman,
who taught me the basic fact of
bulldozer operation:
"Don't bother with all that fancy
stuff, just make it smooth."

First published in 1994 by Motorbooks International Publishers & Wholesalers, PO Box 2, 729 Prospect Avenue, Osceola, WI 54020 USA

© Robert N. Pripps, 1994

Library of Congress Cataloging-in-Publication Data Available

ISBN 0-87938-912-5

On the front cover: This Caterpillar Twenty Two, serial number 1J1507SP, was built in 1937 on 40in gauge tracks. The 251ci overhead-valve engine was rated at 23.43 drawbar horsepower during Nebraska Tests in 1934 using distillate fuel. The Twenty Two is virtually the same as the Caterpillar R2, except that while the R2 used gasoline, most Twenty Twos used distillate. This Twenty Two belongs to Marvin Fery, owner of Marvin Fery Excavation of Salem, Oregon. Marvin is also president and one of the founders of the Antique Caterpillar Machinery Owner's Club.

On the back cover: A 1945 John Deere BO Lindeman Crawler. John Deere BO (Orchard) tractors were converted to crawler tracks by the Lindeman Brothers of Yakima, Washington. Lindeman Crawlers, as they came to be known, were just right for the hilly apple orchards in the Northwest. This 1945 Model BO Lindeman is owned by Harold Schultz of Ollie, Iowa.

On the frontispiece: A 1934 Caterpillar Diesel Seventy Five. The Diesel Seventy Five was the forerunner of the RD8 and the D8. It was powered by a 5.25x8.00in bore and stroke six-cylinder engine. It weighed about 40,000lb, had a six-roller undercarriage, a gear-driven fan, and used a vertical two-cylinder starting motor. There was no electrical system. The Diesel Seventy Five shown is owned by the Skirvin Brothers of Philomath, Oregon. This tractor, serial number 2E46, farmed in Northern California, pulling plows and running a generator set via the belt pulley. It also spent some time pulling excavation scrapers for irrigation. Carl Skirvin recounted the delivery of the first Diesel Seventy Five by train to his area. The price in 1934 was $4,300, equivalent today to about $275,000. He said all the farmers and loggers in the area turned out to see it unloaded.

On the title pages: Marv Fery of Salem, Oregon, tracks his 1935 Caterpillar Twenty Eight under threatening clouds. The Twenty Eight has a wide-gage (55in) track, and a 4.50x5.50in bore and stroke gasoline four-cylinder engine. It is equipped with a factory-installed electric starter. In the process of restoration, Marv overhauled the engine and changed the track rails and bolts, but kept the original pads. This Twenty Eight is serial number 4F929SP.

Printed and bound in Hong Kong

Contents

Foreword

The first vehicle I remember driving (I was about 9 years old at the time) was an Allis-Chalmers crawler. My Dad was discing a fire lane, and I was along for the ride. I suppose he got bored with it, and so, offered me the controls. The feeling of irresistible power got hold of me then, and has never let go.

I don't have a crawler of my own—yet. (My wife says that if I buy one more tractor....) Owning a crawler takes quite a bit more commitment than does a wheel tractor. They seem always to be too heavy for your trailer and pickup; they chew up your turf, driveway, and cement; and something always seems to be wearing out in the rollers or track pins. Nevertheless, if the right D2 or D4 comes along....

In doing this book with Andrew Morland (who is, as you will see, an outstanding photographer), I got to meet some serious crawler tractor collectors, and to see some nicely restored tractors. Andrew and I traveled the United States and Great Britain for photo subjects. Crawler collecting is in its infancy, com-pared to wheel tractors, so finding examples of each type was not easy.

This book is mainly a picture book. But around the pictures I have attempted to hang a framework of history and technical description. It was my goal to show the important part played by the crawler in agriculture, and also to point out how the crawler contributed militarily and in logging and construction.

The book is dedicated to my uncle, Norman E. Pripps, a cat skinner from back before most of us remember, but I also want to acknowledge the hearty souls whose tractors grace these pages. Without their appreciation of this fine old machinery and their devotion to their hobby this book would not have been possible.

Thanks as well to Joycelyn Luster, Archivist for Caterpillar Incorporated; Kelly Kravig, Product Specialist for Case-International; and Katherine Wright and Chuck Kilbreath of Patton Tractor and Equipment of Rockford, Illinois, a Caterpillar dealership.

I also want to extend my thanks to the staff of Motorbooks International and Editor in Chief Michael Dregni. Their work speaks for itself in the following pages.

Robert N. Pripps

1934 Allis-Chalmers Model K Crawler
This Model K is owned by Alan Draper of Great Britain. The Model K was originally developed as the Monarch 35; however, Allis-Chalmers acquired the Monarch Tractor Company in 1928 and changed its designation. The Model K weighs just over 5 tons.

Circa 1943, the author, age 11, hands in pockets, watches Emil Shedell (on tractor) and Bill Saltenberger make ready to contain a forest fire. The tractor, a Cletrac 20 of about 1936 vintage, pulled a large middle-buster plow to make a fire break. The truck is a 1942 Ford. Saltenberger and Shedell worked for the author's father, Raymond Pripps, who was a Wisconsin Conservation Department Forest Ranger. In those days before liability lawsuits were common, the author often "went along" on such operations.

Chapter 1

The Origins of Tracklaying Tractors

*If you wish to hold the load with the machine, draw back the reverse lever toward center and
watch the action of the drive members (tracks). Don't use steam, and don't allow the
[tracks] to stop. These suggestions will be readily understood after a few runs.*
—Running hints for going downhill,
from the *Lombard Log Hauler* manual, circa 1905

Metallurgy, the science and technology of metals, has been the pacing item in the progress of non-animal power. Metallurgy has been the main factor in the process of engine making from the era of early steam to modern-day gas turbine jets. In the Eighteenth Century, the use of iron to make steam engines finally came to fruition. The problem was weight. These early engines were limited to stationary duties, because the strength of the iron dictated great thicknesses.

The idea of self-propelling these early steamers of course came up. Because of the weight-per-horsepower ratio, the first propulsion steam applications were for boats. In 1707, Denis Papin launched his four-paddle paddle wheel boat in Germany. Then came George Stephen-

son in Great Britain and Robert Fulton in America with steam-powered ships. Next, steam power was transferred to rails.

By 1775, the science of metallurgy had progressed to where the thickness of

1926 Caterpillar Sixty
The Cat Sixty began life as the Best Sixty in 1919. It was an immediate success as it was well balanced and reliable. Along with the Best Thirty, the Sixty made such inroads into the sales of Holt tractors that the merger of the two companies was effected in 1925. About the only change made to the Sixty as a result of the merger was the addition of "Caterpillar" to the radiator shell. Production continued through 1931 with some modernization although the crowbar starting arrangement was retained to the end. This Sixty is owned and was restored by Dave Smith of Woodburn, Oregon. Dave is the Treasurer and one of the founders of the Antique Caterpillar Machinery Owner's Club.

1869 Minnis Steam Crawler
The Minnis steam crawler was demonstrated in Ames, Iowa, in 1869. Material shortcomings in that period inhibited successful crawler development. *Caterpillar, Inc.*

STRATTON'S TRACTION ENGINE.

1893 Stratton Steam Traction Crawler
Charles H. Stratton's steam traction crawler was developed in 1893 in Moscow, Pennsylvania. It was a two-cylinder affair with the cold water tank in front of the boiler. *Caterpillar, Inc.*

the metal in a steam engine, and the pressure at which it could operate, allowed weights reasonable for land vehicles. In 1771, Nicolas Joseph Cugnot, a Frenchman, was able to make a steam truck. Cugnot's steam wagon was not, however, a complete success. While it was able to haul a payload, Cugnot had failed to provide an effective means of steering.

Genuinely successful traction engines would have to wait until the mid-

point of the Nineteenth Century. From then until the end of the century, steam tractors reigned supreme. In their heyday, steam traction engines were made that developed 150hp. While there were many brands of steamers, they all had one thing in common: they were heavy. Steam engines, at the turn of this century, and indeed the gasoline/kerosene tractors that were beginning to replace them, weighed over 500lb per drawbar horsepower.

Increasing Tractor Footprint

It is obvious that a 50,000lb tractor is going to sink into soft plowed ground. Indeed, unless the wheels are large and wide, it will sink into firm sod. The

largest engines of the day had drive wheels 9ft in diameter and 3ft in width. This means of spreading the weight over a larger area reached its extreme in a 1900 machine built by Best Manufacturing Company of Stockton, California. Best's 82,000lb machine had drive wheels (made from wood planks, like barrels) that each measured 9ft in diameter and 15ft wide.

No matter what the diameter of the wheel, it makes point contact with a flat surface. Even with railroad wheels and tracks there is some deflection of both surfaces that spreads out the load. This is one of the main benefits of pneumatic tires; they deflect easily and increase the "footprint" area. With steel wheels on a

10

traction engine, almost all of the deflection is in the ground. It does not take much indentation of the soil to increase the rolling friction by a large amount.

Ideas to increase the footprint area over that which could be provided by wheels occurred in several forms. One was horizontal cylinders mounted longitudinally beneath the vehicle. Corkscrew ridges were wrapped around the cylinders with opposite leads. As the cylinders were rotated in opposite directions, the vehicle "screwed itself along the ground" with the weight supported

over the length of the cylinders. Actually, the screw-drive machines worked quite well on snow and ice, but were not efficient on bare ground.

A second method of increasing footprint area was the walking tractor, or wheel-type tracklayer, as pioneered by Boydell in Britain in 1846 and developed by Altgeld in the United States in 1916. The Altgeld version used large drive wheels as on a conventional tractor, but in place of the wheel rim, a flat, hinged plate was attached to the end of each spoke. Each plate had an area of

Caterpillar R4
This dramatic photo shows a Cat R4 pulling a Holt "hillside" combine. The R4 was a development of the Caterpillar Thirty. The designation was changed after about 900 were built. The Thirty was completely new when introduced in 1935. It had a four-cylinder engine of 4.25x5.50in bore and stroke. The big change was that the name on the top of the radiator was changed from "Thirty" to "Caterpillar." The designation "R4" was on the bottom side of the radiator. The Thirty had two top rollers, whereas the R4 (and subsequent D4) had only one.
Deere & Company

11

1949 Caterpillar D4 Ad
"Plowing through 100 miles of drifts," this Caterpillar ad from the November 1949 issue of *Capper's Farmer* magazine touts the capability of the D4.

about 150sq-in. The tractor effectively stepped from one plate to the next.

The crawler, or endless-tracklayer, was also a concept of the 1850s. Again, metallurgy was the pacing item, as successful crawlers were to elude inventors until the end of the century. There were several problems. The first was getting track-link hinge pins to withstand the grit of running in the dirt. Second was getting a track that would stay on its drive and anti-drive wheels while making a turn or operating on a hillside. A third problem was track tensioning. Without the proper tension, the problem of the track coming off in turns was exacerbated.

The earliest endless-track machine seems to be the Minnis Steam Crawler, demonstrated in Ames, Iowa, in 1869. The second was the Stratton Steamer of 1893. The first crawler to find routine employment was the Lombard Log Hauler, a 100hp steam half-track with a ski front end, patented in 1900.

The Lombard Log Hauler weighed over 40,000lb in working trim. Its track area was 1696sq-in. The front skis had an area of about 700sq-in, for a total of 2400sq-in to support the weight, or between 16lb and 17lb per sq-in of footprint pressure. It is interesting to note that the original Lombards were steered by a team of horses hitched to the runners. Later, a steering wheel arrangement was added, and the "pilot" sat in front where the horse driver had been; the engineer was back in the cab with the fireman where he handled the throttle and reversing (brakes) controls.

As many as 200 Log Haulers were made before 1920. They hauled six to ten log sleds over iced roads from the timber to the railhead. The sleds carried an average 6,000 board feet of logs and weighed about 30 tons. The loaded rate of travel was 2mph.

Next page
International Harvester T-4, T-5, and TD-5 Brochure
As this brochure promised, there was an IHC crawler "For every farm use."

NEW

3 MODELS
2 GASOLINE
1 DIESEL

INTERNATIONAL
Farm Crawlers

T-4 Gasoline
34.0 Flywheel—26.3 Drawbar
Horsepower*

T-5 Gasoline
40.0 Flywheel—30.9 Drawbar
Horsepower*

TD-5 Diesel
37.0 Flywheel—28.5 Drawbar
Horsepower*

*Estimated

INTERNATIONAL
HARVESTER

For Every Farm Use

Chapter 2

Development of Tracklayers 1900-1960

*Vast wheat ranches gave rise to stories that a man could start planting at one end
of a tract and harvest on the return trip.*
—The Caterpillar Story

By the year 1900, well over a hundred patents had been issued for tracklaying machines. The logging half-track steamers were the first to attain a measure of success. This was partly due to the benign conditions imposed on the tracks by the ice roads. Agriculture still relied on conventional wheel-type machines.

The size and weight of farm steam traction engines relegated them mainly to the Great Plains of Canada and the United States, and to the huge farms in California and Oregon. Some were to be found in the East and Midwest, of course, but they were mainly used in threshing rings and for land clearing.

In Europe and the American East, steam engines were used to plow smaller farms using the cable and drum method. Engines with built-in cable reels were stationed on either side of a field. The engines would pull the cable

1945 John Deere BO Lindeman Crawler
John Deere BO (Orchard) tractors were converted to crawler tracks by the Lindeman Brothers of Yakima, Washington. Lindeman Crawlers, as they came to be known, were just right for the hilly apple orchards in Washington and Oregon. The low stance, freedom from protrusions above the hood, and the hillside stability made the Lindemans a good seller. This immaculate 1945 Model BO Lindeman is owned by Harold Schultz of Ollie, Iowa.

back and forth dragging a conventional surrey plow with it. In this way, the weight of the engines was kept on firmer surfaces.

Land in California was plentiful and fertile, with a long growing season. Both horses and manpower were scarce, however, and the large California farms (as large as 36,000 acres) used copious amounts of both. Much of the best farmland was reclaimed from the Sacramento River delta. It was soft and spongy peat, rich and black. But it was so boggy that even the horses were shod with fan-like "tule" shoes. This was the land that spawned the crawler farm tractor.

There were 166 American tractor manufacturers listed for 1920, ten of which built crawlers. Although the crawler was increasingly employed in construction, its main uses were still agriculture and logging.

Following World War I, the ancillary elements of the internal-combustion engine rapidly moved toward maturity. That is, carburetors, spark plugs, magnetos, bearings, and the like, were soon brought to a state where improvements over the next decades were evolutionary instead of revolutionary. The tractor received the benefits of the burgeoning automobile industry and it, too, rapidly matured. One item that pushed the tractor toward maturity was the Nebraska Test Law.

The University of Nebraska Tractor Tests
Early farmers were more often than not the victims of over-sold, under-designed tractors. Dissemination of information in the late 1800s and early 1900s was nothing like we enjoy today. Unless someone in your neighborhood had a particular type of tractor, you were not likely to hear much about it. Being rural meant being isolated. Newspapers came by mail several days after the publishing date. Radio was in its infancy. Publication of farming journals was just beginning. And finally, there were no standards by which mechanical things could be measured.

Because there were so many farmers in those days, they had particular clout with the legislatures. Farmers began to clamor for a national rating system for tractors, so that at least the power capability of a tractor could be understood. Competitive tractor trials in Winnipeg and at certain other cities in the United States and Canada pointed out disparities between advertising claims and actual performance. These trials left much to be desired, as the tractors were often heavily modified by the factory and an army of mechanics and engineers kept them running long enough to compete. National legislation became bogged down in politics, however, and never came to pass.

1945 John Deere BO Lindeman Crawler
Harold Schultz and his son-in-law, David Silvers, did the restoration work, both cosmetic and mechanical. Lindeman Crawlers were made from John Deere Model BO wheel tractors shipped to Lindeman in Yakima, Washington, *sans* wheels.

A Nebraska farmer named Wilmot F. Crozier, who had also been a school teacher (to support the farm, he said), purchased a "Ford" tractor from the Minneapolis outfit not related to Henry Ford. The tractor was so unsatisfactory that he demanded the company replace it. They did, but the replacement was worse. Farmer Crozier then bought a Bull tractor. This too was completely unsatisfactory. Next, he bought a 1918 Rumely "Three-plow." The Rumely met, and even exceeded, Crozier's expecta-

tions. Not only did it stand up to the strains of farming, it was able to regularly pull a five-bottom plow. Shortly afterward, Crozier was elected to the Nebraska legislature.

In 1919, Representative Crozier and Senator Charles Warner introduced legislation that resulted in the "Nebraska Test Law." The law required that any tractor sold in the state of Nebraska had to be certified by the state, which was to test the tractors to see that they lived up to their advertised claims. The tests were to be conducted by the University of Nebraska, Agricultural Engineering Department. L. W. Chase and Claude Shedd devised the tests and the test equipment, which have since become standards for the world. The tests had a profound impact on both the quality of tractors and on their acceptance by the farmers of the

1920s. Some of the early crawler-building companies did not continue into the 1930s, partly because of the requirements of the tests and partly because of the post-World War I economic downturn and the fierce competition it engendered.

The year 1940 ushered in perhaps the most profound decade in American history. Some say it saw America at its best. To others it was a time of great national crises having mostly to do with World War II. The 1930s had been a low point for the country because of the grinding depression and the vagaries of wind and weather. Unemployment had gradually diminished over the decade, except for a time in 1938 when it again rose above 10 million. From that time on, war orders brought unemployment to zero. Wages and prices held steady.

The 1930s also saw the beginning of serious conservation efforts. These took the form of public works projects such as forestry, dam building, and the creation of national parks. By 1940, these efforts were beginning to pay off. The economy was improving even as the war clouds grew darker and heavier.

With the decade of the 1940s barely underway, President Franklin Roosevelt,

during one of his memorable "fireside chats," pledged that the United States would become the world's "Arsenal of Democracy." To many, war with the Axis powers was inevitable, so the more help that could be given to the Allies the better. The Lend-Lease Act dispelled all pretenses of neutrality.

All these things worked together to help return the American tractor indus-

1939 Caterpillar R2
The R2 was much the same as the Caterpillar Twenty Two. One of the differences is shown in this photo: the cast-iron track guards on the R2 versus sheet-metal guards on the Twenty Two. This one belongs to Marv Fery of Salem, Oregon.

17

1935 Allis-Chalmers Model L
The Model L was a 22,000lb monster powered first by a six-cylinder Continental engine, but this was soon replaced by a six-cylinder Allis-Chalmers engine of 844ci. Maximum brake horsepower produced during the Nebraska Tests was 91.93. This 1935 model is owned by Norm Meinert of Davis, Illinois.

try to prosperity. When the United States entered the war in December 1941, crawler tractor production was already near maximum capacity. Immediately, models not essential to the war effort were dropped in favor of those that were. Olive drab paint replaced the firm's traditional colors. Plants went on a six-day, three-shift week with employees volunteering for an extra four-hour "Victory Shift." Vacations were suspended; with

gas rationing, there was no place to go anyway. In many of the plants the employees were 80 percent women, so new methods had to be developed to eliminate heavy lifting.

Since few new machines were available for civilian use, dealers turned to rebuilding for their source of income. In that way, needed heavy equipment for the civilian side of the war effort was supplied.

1932 McCormick-Deering T-40 TracTracTor
The T-40 appeared in 1932 and was produced through 1939. It used a six-cylinder engine of 279ci, the same as that of the W-40 wheel tractor. Rated brake horsepower was 43.33. The T-40 weighed 10,790lb for its Nebraska Test in October of 1932. This T-40 is owned by Ike Martyn of Edgar, Wisconsin.

1959 John Deere Model 440
Author Robert N. Pripps maneuvers brother-in-law Joe Lohmeier's John Deere 440 bulldozer opening sugar bush trails. The 440 is a 1959 model. The two-cylinder vertical engine provides about 32hp from 113ci. The crawler weighs about 7,500lb with the dozer blade.

1935 Caterpillar RD6
The RD6 replaced the Diesel Forty, of which only a few were built. It used the same three-cylinder engine of 55hp. The RD6 weighed about 7 tons. This 1935 model is owned by Dave Smith of Woodburn, Oregon.

Caterpillar D4
An armor-plated D4 Caterpillar advances with the troups during World War II. This photo was taken on New Georgia Island in the Solomons. The reliability and performance of the Caterpillar in the military did much to enhance the company's reputation among the service men. Because the crawler was generally paired with a bulldozer blade, servicemen took to calling the whole outfit a bulldozer. The name has mostly stuck. *Caterpillar, Inc.*

Chapter 3

Holt, Best, and Caterpillar

*The Caterpillar Tractor, born of the brain of Benjamin Holt, straightened roads, leveled valleys,
flattened mountains, stored waters, cleared jungles and served our
National Defense. Its crawler track has carried the burdens of mankind and produced food
for the mouths of the world.*
—From a plaque identifying Benjamin Holt's home in Stockton, California

Holt Manufacturing Company

C. H. Holt & Company was started by Charles Holt in San Francisco in 1865. The Holt family had a lumber business back in New Hampshire. The Holts shipped seasoned hardwoods around the horn of South America for use in making wagons and the like in California. The name of the company was changed to Holt Brothers when Charles' brothers, William, Frank, and Benjamin, became partners.

In 1883, the Holt Brothers established the Stockton Wheel Company in Stockton, California, with young Ben as president. Stockton's location on the edge of the fertile delta made it a promising center for farming and commerce.

The dry California climate lent itself to a profound phenomenon at the turn of the century. Wheat could be allowed to ripen on the stalk and the "traveling combined harvester thresher," or combine, could harvest and immediately thresh it. Although these new machines

took up to forty horses and a dozen men to operate, they still offered savings in time and personnel. Because they were needed in the Stockton area, and because they were made of hardwood, the Stockton Wheel Company began marketing a combine of its own design.

The vast numbers of horses required for the combines prompted Ben Holt to become interested in the steam traction engine and development was begun in 1890. In 1892, the company's name was changed to The Holt Manufacturing Company. At the turn of the century, Holt could see that crawler tracks were needed to support the weight. His first crawler was demonstrated in 1904 and went into production soon thereafter. The success of the Holt design is credited to the firm's experience with link-belt chains used in its combines.

As the Holt steam crawler was returning from its successful field demonstration in 1904, a news photographer was heard to say, "She crawls along like a caterpillar." Benjamin Holt was struck by the aptness of the expression and registered the name Caterpillar as a trademark soon after.

By the year 1907, Holt made the switch to internal-combustion engines. The first model had a 40hp overhead-valve four-cylinder gasoline engine. It had a two-speed transmission with a planetary reverse.

Benjamin Holt
Holt was one of the founders of Caterpillar's predecessor companies. According to Reynold M. Wik, in his book *Benjamin Holt & Caterpillar: Tracks & Combines*, Holt's achievements stand in importance with the contributions of Cyrus McCormick, John Deere, and Henry Ford to the history of technology in rural America. Holt was the first to apply the term "Caterpillar." *Caterpillar, Inc.*

Caterpillar Ten

Manufactured from 1928 to 1933, the Model Ten was of the first two small Cats. The other was the Fifteen. Both used a 3.37x4.00in bore and stroke L-head gasoline engine. The Ten weighed about 4,400lb, and was offered in regular and high clearance models. This Ten is owned by Marv Fery of Salem, Oregon.

Best Steamer
Extension wheels were fitted to Holt and Best steam traction engines in an effort to support their great weight in the soft river delta soil around Stockton, California. It appears, from this photo of a Best Steamer taken around the turn of the century, that the extensions were not long enough. The steamer has become mired. One wonders what you used to pull something like this out? *Caterpillar, Inc.*

Success in the West prompted Holt to consider the sales potential of the Midwest and the Great Plains. Transportation costs hampered development of that potential, so Benjamin Holt dispatched his nephew, Pliny Holt, to survey manufacturing sites. He settled on a location near Minneapolis. When this news got out, Murray Baker (a farm implement dealer in Peoria, Illinois) got word to Pliny Holt about a new factory in East Peoria that had just been abandoned by a bankrupt steam engine manufacturer. Holt visited the plant, which was near the Illinois River, and liked what he saw.

In 1909, Holt bought the plant from the bankrupt Colean steam traction engine manufacturing company of East Peoria, Illinois. Production continued at

Stockton as the East Peoria plant came online. Both factories were building the Holt Model 60 and 75 machines. Murray Baker joined the firm becoming vice president and general manager of the new plant.

A feature of Holt's Caterpillar was the clutch arrangement. A master clutch was used between the engine and transmission. Track clutches disconnected individual tracks to allow steering by a tiller wheel out in front. Thus, a differential was not needed. This clutch configuration has been the hallmark of Caterpillar tractors ever since, although individual track brakes were subsequently added, which eventually eliminated the tiller wheel. Other brands of crawlers also used this method. It is interesting to note that Holt obtained a patent for this system of clutches in 1891.

Holt prospered during World War I, building several models for domestic and export trade. At Holt's urging, the US Army began employing crawler tractors as foreign militaries had done in the war. The US Army, in typical fashion, would not take in-production machines, but wanted new designs. Accordingly, Holt designed two new tractors: the 5-

Daniel Best
Best was another one of the founders of the companies that became Caterpillar, followed his brothers west from Iowa in 1859. After several years of prospecting, and a stint as a sawmill operator in Oregon, Daniel joined one of his brothers in California, doing what they knew best: wheat farming. Daniel Best had an inventive turn of mind. He patented a grain cleaner and a "traveling combined harvester thresher" before becoming involved with steam engines. The first engine to bear his name came out in 1889. Within two years, he had sold twenty-five engines. Because of the great weight of the steamers, crawler tracks were soon fitted. Daniel Best and Ben Holt for years wrangled over combine and steam engine patents and for market share. Finally in 1908, Best sold out to Holt. *Caterpillar, Inc.*

Ton T-11 and the 10-Ton T-16. These were the products with which Holt entered the 1920s.

The third crawler tested at the University of Nebraska was the Holt T-11, tested from August 30 to September 17, 1920. It was considerably bigger than the Cletrac and Monarch already tested, weighing in at 9,400lb. The engine was Holt's own four-cylinder design of 425ci.

The Holt 10-Ton, or T-16, was also tested at Nebraska at about the same time as the 5-Ton. The Holt-built four-cylin-

der engine in the 10-Ton displaced 929ci.

Holt brought out its T-35 model in 1921 as a 4,000lb machine, later to be renamed the 2-Ton. The 276ci four-cylinder engine featured an overhead cam.

Although Holt had prospered during the war, the end of the war left the company foundering. Almost half of Holt's wartime production had been exported; with the war's end, most outstanding orders were canceled. Holt's dealer and service people had not benefited from the foreign sales and were left

somewhat unprepared to compete with Best. Finally, in 1920, in the midst of the postwar depression, the venerable Benjamin Holt died. Holt's business manager, an iron-fisted Bostonian named Thomas Baxter, took over. Baxter paired the larger models from the line and aimed marketing efforts more at construction than agriculture.

The Best Manufacturing Company

The California Gold Rush dramatically changed the state in the year 1849. Nothing moves men like the smell of

1894 Best Steam Traction Engine

The Best steam traction engine, as shown here, was gear driven, while the Holt used a chain drive. Originally intended for agricultural use, the steamers soon found use in logging. This photo was taken in 1894. Things have changed a lot in 100 years of timber harvesting, but it is still hard, dangerous, and equipment-intensive work. *Caterpillar, Inc.*

gold and the population of "The Golden State" burgeoned. Only a few actually found the precious metal, so most of those who stayed in the Golden State

1908 Holt No. 122 Steam Crawler
The Holt No. 122 steam crawler of 1908 demonstrated the benefits of crawlers in earth-moving. It was first used in building the Los Angeles Aqueduct. *Caterpillar, Inc.*

reverted to the trades they had known before.

One of those who went west for gold was Daniel Best. He followed his brothers, leaving his Iowa farm home in the year 1859. After several years of prospecting to no avail, and a stint as a sawmill operator in Oregon, Daniel joined one of his brothers in what they knew from Iowa: wheat farming.

Daniel Best had an inventive turn of mind. When he saw the time and ex-

pense in hauling the newly harvested grain to a central cleaning station, he set about building a small portable field cleaner. The Best grain cleaner was patented in 1871. Initially, the cleaners were made in Oakland, California, but soon better quarters were available in nearby San Leandro.

As the "traveling combined harvester threshers" made their appearance on the California scene, Best became interested in building one of his own, incorporating his patented cleaner. The Best combine went on the market in 1885.

During his time in Oregon, Daniel met a steam engine designer named De Lafayette Remington. Remington's engines had met with considerable success

in the Oregon logging operations. In 1887, Remington's factory in Oregon burned down. Rather than rebuild, Remington drove his remaining engine to San Leandro. Here he demonstrated the engine to Daniel Best and then sold him his patents. Now Best was also in the steam engine business. The first engine to bear his name came out in 1889. Within two years, he had sold twenty-five engines for logging and farm use.

The time around the dawn of the Twentieth Century was a time of turmoil in American industry. Economic times were hard and competition was fierce. Many industrialists sought relief from the intense competition by merging with their competitors. These years also saw the rise of trust-busting politicians.

Daniel Best and Ben Holt went through these times and for years they wrangled over combine and steam engine patents as they battled for market share. Finally, in 1908, Best, now 70 years of age, sold out to Holt. One of the terms of the sale, however, was that Clarence Leo Best, Daniel's son, would buy into the company and be named manager of the San Leandro plant.

C. L. Best Gas Traction Company

C. L. Best worked for Holt for two years. It was said that he never paid for his share of the company, and that his position at the San Leandro plant was not what he had hoped. In 1910, Best left the Holt company and started C. L. Best Gas Traction Company on money borrowed from his father. Starting in Elmhurst, California, C. L. Best pro-

duced wheel-type internal-combustion traction engines for farm work. Almost immediately, he also went to work on a crawler. In 1913, the C.L.B. 75 "Tracklayer" was announced with a 70hp internal-combustion engine.

Best trademarked the name "Tracklayer," to counter Holt's Caterpillar. His machines featured a number of improvements. Notable was the track-pivoting mechanism that greatly reduced shock loads on the frame and engine. His machines also incorporated a differential, rather than steering clutches as in the Holt design. Best dropped the tiller-wheel steering method in 1914.

Best came into the decade of the 1920s with two sturdy models: the Sixty and the Thirty. The Sixty was introduced in 1919 and was tested at Nebraska in 1921. Getting the Sixty through the

1913 Best 75
Best used the name "Tracklayer" to counter Holt's "Caterpillar" trademark. The Best 75 of 1913 was the first to use the Tracklayer name. *Caterpillar, Inc.*

tests was not as easy as might have been anticipated. It was apparent by then to the Best staff that the 1128ci four-cylinder engine was not likely to reach its 60hp rating claim. For the testing, Best removed the air cleaner in an effort to raise the output, and consequently, the tractor had to be sold in Nebraska without one. Nevertheless, the tractor only achieved a power rating of 55hp. The tractor weighed 17,500lb for the tests.

The Best Thirty was presented in 1921 and was originally sold under the name Best Model S. It was about a half-

1915 Best Pony
The 1915 Best Pony, or "Muley" Tracklayer, had a 16hp engine. Of Best and Holt, Best was the first to drop the front tiller wheel. The grim look on the face of the operator probably means he has just realized that the wheel of the implement has gone on the wrong side of the tree. *Caterpillar, Inc.*

scale version of the Sixty. The four-cylinder engine displaced 675ci, and the weight was about 7,400lb. Like the Sixty, the Thirty was tested at Nebraska in May 1921. Achieving the 30hp rating was not easy for this model, either. The tests were conducted at 10rpm over the normal 800, the ignition timing was advanced 5 degrees, and the carburetor was enlarged. Even at that, the rated horsepower and the maximum available

horsepower were virtually the same. By now, Best tractors used steering clutches and brakes, rather than differential steering. On the low-seat models the steering clutch levers extended out to the right. The handles were above the right fender so that the operator could activate them with his right hand. High-seat models had conventional levers.

The Caterpillar Tractor Company

In April 1925, Holt and Best again combined into a single entity: the Caterpillar Tractor Company of Peoria, Illinois, and San Leandro, California. A subsidiary, the Western Harvester Company, was also formed. Western Harvester made combines in Holt's Stockton, California, plant. The merger of these two crawler pioneers made formi-

dable competition for the others. A network of eighty-nine dealers was forged out of the best of both of the old companies. The Best Sixty and Thirty were carried over by the new company and made in the San Leandro plant. The Holt 2-Ton, 5-Ton, and 10-Ton Models were continued in Peoria.

The first new tractor under the Caterpillar banner was the Twenty, which made its debut to replace the 2-Ton in 1927. The new company avoided the rating problems faced by Best during the Nebraska Tests by giving its new tractors conservative names. The Twenty was easily capable of producing 29 belt horsepower, and when pulling at 20hp on the drawbar, it exhibited only 0.45 percent slippage.

In 1928, Caterpillar also brought out

Holt Caterpillar 45
The Holt 45 is shown in a plowing demonstration, circa 1916, pulling two John Deere three-bottom plows. Forward visibility was somewhat restricted. *Deere & Company*

two smaller "Cats." These were the Models Ten and Fifteen. Both models used L-head four-cylinder engines of 143ci and 221ci respectively. Weights were 4,575lb for the Ten and 5,931lb for the Fifteen. These were later upgraded: the Ten became the Fifteen, the old Fifteen became the new Twenty, and the old Twenty became the Twenty Five.

In 1928, Caterpillar also bought out the Russell Grader Manufacturing Company of Minneapolis, Minnesota, bringing Caterpillar into the road grader busi-

1919 Best 60
The Best 60, shown in this 1919 photo tanking up at an intown service station, was one of the most successful tractors in this time period. The "convertible" top identifies this as a "Logging Cruiser" model. Note the padded tracks for street use. *Caterpillar, Inc.*

Holt Caterpillar Sixty

Caterpillars (Holts) were sold to the Russians before the Bolshevik Revolution in 1917. This post-revolution shot shows a Holt Caterpillar Sixty. *Caterpillar, Inc.*

Caterpillar Sixty

The Best Sixty became the Caterpillar Sixty following the merger of Best and Holt into Caterpillar in 1925. The one shown is serial number 3331A, and is owned by Dave Smith of Woodburn, Oregon. Dave got it from Francis Meier, a wheat farmer from Davis, California, who also operated a Cat Thirty.

ness. In 1931, Caterpillar brought out its first motor grader. Caterpillar gasoline Twenty Five (the upgrade of the old Twenty) came out in 1933.

The year 1931 was a banner one for Caterpillar, and indeed for the tractor industry as a whole. After two years of secret development, the first diesel tractor to be tested at Nebraska, the "Diesel," or "Diesel Sixty" was introduced. Despite many growing pains, the diesel-powered Caterpillar set new standards for durability and economy. Cat also pioneered the use of a small, independent gasoline engine for starting. The Diesel Sixty became the Diesel Sixty Five. Over the next two years it was joined by the Diesel Thirty Five, the Diesel Fifty, and finally, the Diesel Seventy Five. The Diesel Thirty Five represented a break with Caterpillar tradition in that a three-cylinder engine, rather than a four-cylinder, was used. The engine of the Fifty was the

same bore and stroke (5.25x8.00in), but had four cylinders. The Seventy used the engine of the old Sixty Five in the new larger Seventy Five chassis.

Because they were much cheaper (the Diesel Sixty Five sold for $6,500, a king's ransom in 1932), Caterpillar mainly continued with gasoline engines for a time. The Seventy (gasoline) was about the same size (32,000lb) as the Diesel Seventy Five, but was $2,000 less expensive.

The year 1934 saw the beginning of the switch to letter-number designators for Caterpillar tractors. R was used for gasoline-powered engines as the R2, R4, and R5 were unveiled. The RD designation was reserved for diesels. Also in 1934, a Model Twenty Two appeared. It was essentially the same as the R2, ex-

30

The Caterpillar D8 and the Seabees

My uncle, Norman E. Pripps, to whom this book is dedicated, operated heavy equipment while in the Navy Seabees in World War II. His outfit built airfields and roads in the Solomon and Philippine Islands. He said they had four D8s, several big Allis-Chalmers and some Internationals. He said the D8s lasted throughout the war, while the others were generally replaced after each campaign. He also said that the others needed a "push-cat" to fill a 12-yard scraper, but the D8, by itself, could fill one up and run it over.

Uncle Norman recounted an incident that occurred during the initial landings on Bougainville. The LST he was on could not get close enough to shore to unload tanks directly, so a special ramp was used to carry the tanks and other equipment from the ship to shallow water. To hold the ramp in place during the process, two D8s were driven off into the deep water (with Uncle Norman operating one of them) and maneuvered so that they faced each other on either side of the ramp with their bulldozer blades holding the ramp in place. Uncle Norman said he was up to his midriff in water as he sat on the seat. He said the fan belts had been removed, but otherwise, the D8s had not been modified as far as he knew. He sat aboard his D8, with the engine idling, throughout the entire unloading. When finished, he drove the D8 up on the beach where mechanics changed the oil and sent the D8 on its way for other duties.

Needless to say, the D8 was a favorite with my Uncle Norman. He felt that all other crawlers, except perhaps the D7, were toys.

Caterpillar Sixty

Born as the Best Sixty in 1919, it was the first heavy Best crawler to get along without a tiller wheel for steering. Farmers and loggers considered the Sixty the standard of the industry, and it became a legend in its own time.

cept for a 10in track instead of the 13in track of the R2. The main difference was that the Model Twenty Two was configured for distillate, or tractor, fuel, which was popular at the time with farmers.

In 1935, the Caterpillar (gasoline)

Thirty and Forty, and the Diesel Forty made the scene. The Diesel Forty of 5.25x5.75in bore and stroke used a three-cylinder engine, while the gasoline version used four cylinders. Five of the last Diesel Fortys got the larger (5.75x8.0in) three-cylinder engine destined for the RD6.

The RD4, RD6, RD7, and RD8 models came out in the next year, 1936. The RD4 had a four-cylinder, 4.25x5.50in bore and stroke engine of 40hp. It weighed 5 tons. The three larger models used the same displacement pistons; 5.75x8.00in bore and stroke, but different numbers of cylinders. The RD6 replaced the Diesel Forty and used the

three-cylinder engine with 55hp. It weighed 7 to 8 tons, depending on the track configuration. The RD7 replaced the Diesel Fifty. It used a four-cylinder engine with a rated horsepower of 70hp at 850rpm. It weighed 10 tons. The RD8 replaced the Diesel Seventy Five without much change.

In 1938, the "R" (which some believe stood for Roosevelt) was dropped from the designation of diesel tractors, but retained for gasoline models. The diesels now used D2, D4, D5 (of which only a few were made in 1939), D6, D7, and D8. The D8 (a term which has since come to mean the ultimate) went into

1940 with its six-cylinder engine of 1246ci producing a maximum of 118 brake horsepower at 1000rpm. The weight was 17 tons.

Caterpillar entered the 1940s by increasing the horsepower of its Model D8 and providing it with an oil cooling system. The engine was still the 5.75x8.00in bore and stroke six-cylinder unit, but power was increased through refinements. The D8 continued through 1960 with this engine, but by then it was turbocharged and operated at 1200rpm. The D8 weighed almost 54,000lb and registered a drawbar pull of 45,526lb during its Nebraska Test in 1959.

1926 Caterpillar Sixty
This Cat Sixty spent its working life on a wheat farm near Davis, California. It pulled plows and a Caterpillar Number 36 Combine. It had about 2,000 hours when acquired by Dave Smith of Woodburn, Oregon. It still had the original tracks and the original drawbar and pin. Dave Smith is an accomplished Cat restorer and collector, and an originator of the Antique Caterpillar Machinery Owner's Club. Dave is also the President of TRECO (Oregon Rootstock and Tree Company, Incorporated), a grower of apple trees.

1926 Caterpillar Sixty
Left side of the Sixty's engine. The engine was a four-cylinder of 6.50x8.50in bore and stroke, a total of 1128ci. It was of the overhead-valve type rated at 650rpm. The carburetor is a Stromberg.

The D7 was also uprated for 1940 to a maximum horsepower of 89 at 1000 rpm. The power was produced by the same 5.75x8.00in bore and stroke four-cylinder engine. The D7 was a favorite of the military, because it was the largest dozer that would fit in a smaller landing craft. Many D7s were armor plated for use with the front-line troops. In 1959,

1926 Caterpillar Sixty
Right side of the Sixty's engine. The Bosch magneto and water pump are shown. The four cylinders are cast singly. The engine produces 60 belt horsepower.

1931 Caterpillar Diesel Sixty

One of the first two Caterpillar diesels, mounted in a Sixty chassis, began operating in 1931. It is still operating and is in the hands of a California collector. Early diesels, like early steam engines, were limited to stationary and marine uses because of their weight. Caterpillar began development of the tractor diesel in 1926. *Caterpillar, Inc.*

the D7 produced 110 drawbar horsepower during its Nebraska Test. Since no PTO was fitted, engine power output could not be measured. The 831ci four-

Caterpillar Ten

The Cat Ten was manufactured from 1928 to 1933, and it was the smallest Caterpillar made. This one, serial number 3609, is owned by Marv Fery.

Caterpillar Ten
Marv Fery's Cat Ten has the optional 44in tread. A tread of 37.5in was standard. The Ten is about the same size as the Holt/Caterpillar 2-Ton, but was considerably different.

Caterpillar Ten
The Model Ten made its debut in 1928. It used an L-head four-cylinder engine of 3.37x4.00in bore and stroke, for a displacement of 143ci. Operating speed was 1500rpm.

Russell Grader

The Russell Grader Company was bought out by Caterpillar in 1928. Russell had built a line of versatile pull-type graders for many years. Shown here is the author's medium-size Russell behind his 1948 John Deere B. The grader has been modified so that the tractor's hydraulic lift can raise and lower the blade, eliminating the need for a grader operator.

1930–1931 Caterpillar Twenty

This Twenty was apparently made in the San Leandro plant, as the lettering is in black; Peoria tractors had red lettering. It has a generator, electric start, provisions for lights, and a logging winch. Twentys were made from 1927 through 1931. The Twenty was the first new tractor under the Caterpillar banner after the merger between Holt and Best. It was easily capable of producing 29 belt horsepower and pulling 20hp on the drawbar. Ike Martyn of Edgar, Wisconsin, owns this Caterpillar Twenty. He thinks it is of 1930 or 1931 vintage.

cylinder engine was rated at 1000rpm and was turbocharged.

The Caterpillar D6 was completely redesigned for 1941. A new 4.25x5.50in bore and stroke six-cylinder engine replaced the three-cylinder unit. In appearance, it looked like a small version of the D7. Weighing in at 17,750lb for its Nebraska Test in September 1941, the D6 pulled 16,674lb during the maximum drawbar pull test. Rated belt horsepower was 69 at 1400rpm. The D6 featured hydraulically boosted steering clutches. By 1960, power was increased by running the engine at 1600rpm.

In 1947, Caterpillar upgraded the D2 through D6. The D2 got a new 4.00x 5.00in bore and stroke engine rated at 32 drawbar horsepower. The D4 got a new 4.50x5.50in engine rated at 43 drawbar horsepower. The D6 had a 65 drawbar horsepower six-cylinder version of the 4.50x5.50in engine.

In 1954, these three tractors were again upgraded in power through breathing improvements, compression increases, and by increasing the rated rpm. The D2 was rated at 35, the D4 at 48, and the D6 at 75 drawbar horsepower. There were also R (gasoline versions) of the tractor line from the R2 to the R6, including the little-produced R5. Many components were common to the diesel counterparts. The R6 was the last of the

1939 Caterpillar R2

Marvin Fery's Caterpillar R2 is serial number 6J268SP (Special Purpose). The SP designation could indicate things such as alternate gear ratios or special equipment. Marv is the second owner. He bought the R2 from the Beitel Brothers of Sublimity, Oregon, where it had done row-crop, wheat, and grass farming as well as skidding logs.

big gas crawlers by Caterpillar. Fuel consumption was just too much; a well-loaded R6 could go through 80 gallons of fuel in a day.

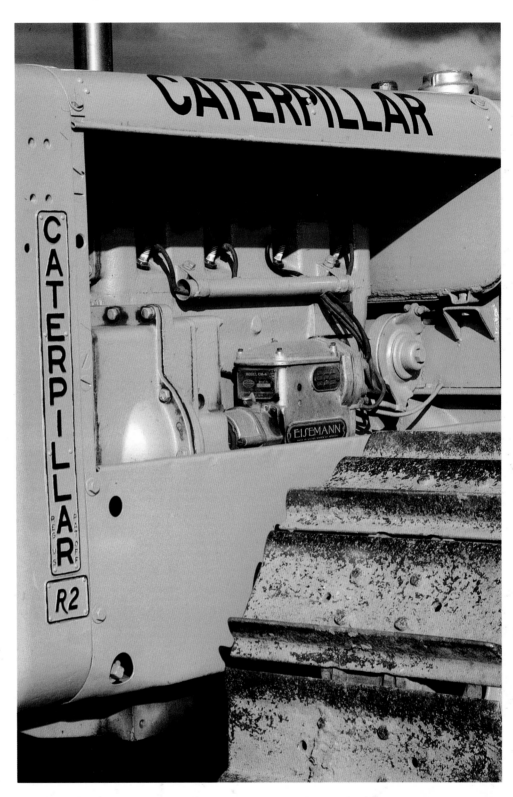

1939 Caterpillar R2
This Cat R2 has the optional 50in track gage; 40in is standard. It is a 1939 model, owned by Marv Fery. The R2 was introduced in 1934. Also in 1934, a Model Twenty Two appeared. It was essentially the same as the R2, except for a 10in track instead of the 13in track of the R2.

1939 Caterpillar R2
The R2 used a four-cylinder engine of 3.75x5.00in bore and stroke. Rated engine speed was 1525rpm. Rated belt horsepower was 25.06, with 31.07hp on the belt. Nominal weight of the R2 was 6,130lb.

Previous page

1935 Caterpillar Twenty Eight
Another of the nifty small Caterpillars, the Twenty Eight was a follow-on to the Twenty Five and the Twenty. It was sold between 1933 and 1935. This one, a 1935 model, is owned by Marvin Fery of Salem, Oregon.

1935 Caterpillar Twenty Eight
The engine of the Twenty Eight produced 30.49hp on the drawbar and 37.47hp on the belt at 1100rpm. The four cylinders had a bore and stroke of 4.19x5.50in.

1935 Caterpillar Twenty Eight
The Cat Twenty Eight had much in common with the R3. The engine of the R3 had a bore of 4.50in rather than 4.19in of the Twenty Eight. Both used the same crankshaft and had 5.50in strokes.

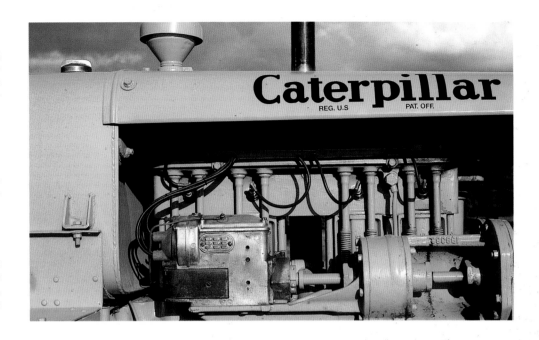

1935 Caterpillar Twenty Eight
Marv Fery's Twenty Eight is the wide gage
(55in) version. It has factory electric start. The
serial number is 4F929SP (Special Purpose).
Since he's owned it, Marv has changed the
rails and bolts, but the pads are original.

1929 Caterpillar Thirty
The Cat Thirty was built from 1921 to 1932. The one shown, serial number 9446, was built in 1929 before the color change to Caterpillar Yellow in March 1931. At first, the steering clutch levers extended out to the right with the handles above the right fender. Later, conventional levers were added.

1931 Caterpillar Thirty
A Caterpillar Thirty halls a train of grain bundle wagons at the Petukhovsky Collective Farm in the USSR, circa 1931. Some of the state farms in the Soviet Union were as large as 400,000 acres. Between October 1929, and May 1930, more than $12 million in sales were made to the USSR. And brisk sales continued for the next several years. This provided Caterpillar with much needed cash to weather the Great Depression. *Caterpillar, Inc.*

1929 Caterpillar Thirty
Marvin Fery, President of the Antique Caterpillar Machinery Owner's Club, drives his 1929 Cat Thirty. It took Marv over a year to restore the Thirty. The engine was stuck, as was the clutch, and there was a lot of rust. The undercarriage, however, was in fine shape.

1929 Caterpillar Thirty
The Thirty was originally sold under the name Best Model S. It was about a half-scale version of the Sixty. The four-cylinder engine displaced 675ci, and the weight was about 7,400lb.

Caterpillar D2
The D2 was one of the best small Cats. It was built from 1938 to 1947, and was popular with farmers. There was a gasoline version, as well, the R2, but it was never sold in the quantities of the D2. Interestingly, the D2 used the same 10hp pony motor as the D4. On the D2 and early D4s the pony exhaust was not used to warm the diesel to aid in starting. This picture shows the fuel injectors of the D2 owned by Loren Fossum of Northfield, Minnesota.

Caterpillar D4
Crawlers, such as this D4, had the power and traction to pull farm equipment such as this ditcher. The D4 from the era of the photo, about 1947, had 35 drawbar horsepower. It had a four-cylinder engine of 4.25x5.50in bore and stroke. *Deere & Company*

1947 Caterpillar D4 Ad
This 1947 Caterpillar ad features a 10-year-old D4. It's from the August issue of *Capper's Farmer.*

1935 Caterpillar RD6
The RD6 replaced the Diesel Forty, and weighed in at 7 tons. The RD6 shown belongs to David B. Smith of Woodburn, Oregon. He estimates it has a total of 16,350 hours.

1935 Caterpillar RD6
Dave Smith of Woodburn, Oregon, aboard his
Caterpillar RD6.

1935 Caterpillar RD6
The RD6 used the three-cylinder 55hp engine from the late-model Caterpillar Forty Diesel. It had a bore and stroke of 5.75x8.00in.

1936 Caterpillar RD6
Dave Smith at the crank of his 1936 Model RD6. The crank starts the pony motor, which in turn starts the three-cylinder diesel. He has put on new tracks and new rails as part of his complete restoration.

Next page
1936 Caterpillar RD6
The RD6 was built in model years 1936 through 1938. In 1938, the "R" (which some believe stood for Roosevelt) was dropped from the designation of diesel tractors, but retained for gasoline models. From 1939 to the present time it has been built as the D6. Of course there were many changes and the current model resembles the original in designation, only. For example, in 1941, the three-cylinder engine was replaced with a six-cylinder unit. Dave Smith's 1936 model is shown.

Caterpillar Diesel Forty
The Diesel Forty used a three-cylinder engine. The RD6 replaced the Diesel Forty and also used the three-cylinder engine, which had about 55hp. The Forty is shown pulling a John Deere Reversible Disk plow. *Deere & Company*

1940 Caterpillar D7
This famous dramatic shot shows a D7 clearing London streets of rubble during the Battle of Britain. The D7 for 1940 had maximum power of 89hp at 1000rpm. The power was produced by the same 5.75x8.00in bore and stroke four-cylinder engine. *Caterpillar, Inc.*

1934 Caterpillar Diesel Seventy Five
The massive front end of the Diesel Seventy Five. This was an ideal logging tractor as it could run inexpensively on diesel fuel and skid logs through the toughest terrain.

1934 Caterpillar Diesel Seventy Five
The Diesel Seventy Five began life with the pony motor from the Diesel Seventy, which it replaced. This motor had the same pistons as those of the Caterpillar Ten tractor. Later, a new more-compact, but larger-displacement, two-cylinder pony starting motor was provided.

Caterpillar Diesel Seventy Five
An early Caterpillar Diesel Seventy Five operates a LeTourneau scraper. *Caterpillar, Inc.*

Next page
1934 Caterpillar Diesel Seventy Five
The forerunner of the D8, the Diesel Seventy Five was built from late 1933 to early 1935. It used a 5.25x8in bore and stroke six-cylinder engine operating at 650rpm. It weighed in the neighborhood of 40,000lb. The tractor shown was built in 1934, and looks quite potent for a sixty-year-old machine. It is owned by the Skirvin Brothers of Philomath, Oregon.

Chapter 4

Cletrac, Oliver, and White

This tractor automatically lays and travels on a smooth level track, strong, durable and flexible,
over which it successfully negotiates ploughed fields, soft delta lands, prairies,
country and mountain roads, and operates successfully over field and highway surfaces that are
very difficult to negotiate with wheel traction engines.
—Victor Pagé,
The Modern Gas Tractor: Its Construction, Operation, Application and Repair, 1917

The Cleveland Tractor Company

Thomas H. White, and his three sons Windsor, Walter, and Rollin, typified the inventive genius that was prevalent in America before the dawn of the Twentieth Century. Thomas White made his fortune in the sewing machine business with a machine he invented in about 1859. In the late 1890s, the sons became interested in steam engines and the burgeoning automobile business and their White Steam Car was introduced in 1900. Although the White steamer was quite successful, the trend to internal combustion was obvious, so the brothers began work on an engine of their own design. An offshoot of this effort was the Cleveland Motor Plow Company.

The Cleveland Motor Plow Company was formed in 1911 to build a small crawler tractor for agricultural use. The

1947 Oliver "Cletrac" Model BD

In 1944, the Oliver Farm Equipment Company changed its name to The Oliver Corporation and took over the Cleveland Tractor Company (Cletrac). Production of crawlers continued in Cleveland. The tractor shown is a 1947 model Oliver "Cletrac" BD. A similar version, the Oliver "Cletrac" B, or BG, had a gasoline engine. The BD shown is awaiting restoration by owner John Eggers of Two Rivers, Wisconsin. John is a consummate antique machinery restorer, and is the President of EVM, Incorporated, a maker of machine products.

name of this company was changed to The Cleveland Tractor Company in 1916. The foreshortened version, Cletrac, was registered in 1918.

Cletracs never used a tiller wheel, as did their contemporaries. Instead, they relied on differential steering, as did the C. L. Best tractors. This type of steering functions in the same manner as individual wheel brakes on a conventional wheel-type tractor. Proponents claim advantages for differential steering when descending steep grades or when going across a steep side hill. Clutch-type steering requires de-clutching a track to make a turn, which can allow that track to roll freely, unless the brake is simultaneously applied.

Early Cletracs had a reputation for high power-to-weight ratios, low maintenance, and for good ground clearance. They were also considered to be quite durable. Many production tractors didn't use White-built engines, but those purchased from Weidley, Wisconsin, and Hercules. The White Brothers also went on to produce the White heavy-duty truck.

The first crawler tested by the University of Nebraska was the Cletrac Model W 12-20. Testing was begun on July 29, 1920, and was completed on August 9. The Model W was first introduced in 1919 and remained in production

through 1931. It featured the 277ci four-cylinder Wiedley overhead-valve engine, somewhat larger than that used earlier. The Model W weighed in at just over 3,300lb, and in the maximum drawbar pull test, pulled 1,734lb. The company optimistically estimated a one-acre-per-hour plowing rate using three 14in bottoms. The Model W was built until 1932.

The next Cletrac to be tested at Nebraska was the Model F. A positively remarkable little crawler, the Cletrac Model F was introduced in 1920. This 1900lb tractor could pull 90 percent of its own weight. The unusual (for its day) track system employed "high-drive" sprockets. It also employed a floating roller chain inside each track, which eliminated the need for bogie wheels. Cletrac used its own four-cylinder engine in the Model F, which continued in production through 1922.

The Cletrac Model K was introduced in 1925. It was variously identified as the 15-25, or the 20. The Model K, or K-20 as it was usually called, was improved and modernized over its production life, which lasted to 1932. It was available in either gasoline or kerosene versions. The 4.00x5.50in bore and stroke engine was built by Cletrac. The K-20 was characterized by a seven-roller track, curved-down-at-the-rear fenders, a

1949 Oliver Ad
An Oliver ad from the November 1949 *Capper's Farmer* magazine.

1947 Oliver "Cletrac" Model BD
John Eggers of Two Rivers, Wisconsin, owns this Oliver "Cletrac" Model BD. He bought it in the Delevan, Wisconsin, area, where it had been used in mint farming in the soft gumbo soil.

rear belt pulley, a PTO, and a deep-pan seat.

The 20G replaced the K-20 in 1933. It used a Hercules L-head engine of 4.00x4.50in bore and stroke. A bench seat was now used, as were flat fenders. Steering levers replaced the steering wheel. Production continued through 1935.

In 1925, when the Model K-20 was introduced, a Model 30, or 30-35, was also added to the lineup. It used a 45hp-rated Wisconsin four-cylinder engine. Bore and stroke were 4.00x5.50in. The tractor had a seven-roller undercarriage and used a bench seat. The 30 was built until 1931.

1947 Oliver "Cletrac" Model BD
The 1947 Model BD was powered by a six-cylinder Hercules engine of 38 drawbar horsepower. Twelve-volt electric starting was standard. Advertising claimed it could plow 10 acres in 10 hours on 18 gallons of fuel.

A Model 40 and a Model 100 were added in 1927. Both used six-cylinder engines with electric starting. A Beaver engine was used in the 40 that had a bore and stroke of 4.50x5.00in; the Model 100 had a Wisconsin engine with a bore and stroke of 6.00x7.00in. In 1930, a Hercules engine version of the Model 40 was introduced, called the 40-30. In 1934, Cletrac's first diesel was brought out. It was a version of the 40, called the 40D. It had an electrically started six-cylinder Hercules Diesel of 5.00x6.00in bore and stroke. The Model 100 was dropped from the line in 1930.

Also in 1930, the Cletrac 15 replaced the old 12-20. The 15 used a four-cylinder Hercules engine with a bore and stroke of 4.00x4.50in. After the 12-20

was discontinued, Cletrac no longer built its own engines.

A Model 80-60 also joined the line in 1930, using a 5.50x6.00in six-cylinder Wisconsin engine. Cletrac was now into big tractors, as the 80-60 had a maximum horsepower of 90 and weighed in at almost 23,000lb.

The year 1936 saw a new line of Cletracs with a new designation scheme generally using two letters (there were several exceptions). Included were the AG, BG, BD, CG, DD, FG, FD, HG, and

the smallest Cletrac, the Model E. There were four diesels and eleven gasoline or tractor fuel models. Power ranged from 22 to 94hp. The largest Cletrac, the Model FD, was about the same size and power as the new Cat D8 and the Allis-Chalmers L. Most of these models featured new "streamlined" styling by designer Lawrence Blazey that was quite advanced for the day. They were all built into the 1940s.

Interestingly, a few years later in 1939, Cletrac introduced the Model GG. It was the only wheel-type tractor ever built by Cletrac. Called the General, it was marketed by Cletrac and Massey

Harris until 1942. The General was then sold to B. F. Avery.

Oliver-Cletrac

Cletrac went into the 1940s with a lineup of seven crawler models. They were the Models A through H, omitting the G, which was a wheel tractor. The second letter of the model designation indicated gasoline or diesel, except when it was a high clearance model; then an H was the second letter and the G or D was last.

In 1944, the Oliver Farm Equipment Company changed its name to The Oliver Corporation and took over the Cleve-

1920–1922 Cletrac Model F
The Model F was introduced in 1920. This 1900lb tractor could pull 90 percent of its own weight. Notice the "high-drive" sprockets. It also employed a floating roller chain inside each track, which eliminated the need for bogie wheels.

land Tractor Company. Production of crawlers continued in Cleveland. The previous line was continued, except the AG-6 was added and the FD was dropped (an FDE was added in 1945).

In 1951, a new designation scheme was initiated. An "OC" designation, for Oliver-Cletrac, was used. The OC-3 re-

1920–1922 Cletrac Model F
Cletrac used its own four-cylinder engine in the Model F, which was produced from 1920 through 1922. Notice that the belt pulley extends from the front of the engine: one can imagine the trouble in lining up a belt and getting it tight.

Oliver "Cletrac" Model OC-3
The Oliver "Cletrac" Model OC-3 was a lightweight, small-farm machine, capable of pulling two 14in plows. This one has a nice front-end loader installed.

Oliver "Cletrac" Model OC-3
Ev Warner of Springstead, Wisconsin, has owned this OC-3 for many years. It is not a collector's item, but a work tractor that gets a lot of use.

placed the HG and was virtually identical to it. An all new OC-18 came out with an 895ci Hercules six-cylinder diesel rated at 130hp. It had a unique system of steering clutches and brakes with four steering levers and two brake pedals. The outside lever declutched and braked the corresponding track allowing for spot turns. The inside lever caused a half step power shift ratio increase for the corresponding track, causing it to run slower than the opposite track, for sweeping turns. Both inside

levers could be pulled together for a "Torque-Amplifier" type of downshift. The foot (air) brakes could also be used for turning.

Based on the Oliver 77 wheel tractor, a crawler Model OC-6 was introduced in 1954. The Oliver 194ci six-cylinder engine was used and was available in either diesel or gasoline versions. The tractor weighed just under 7,000lb.

Also in 1954, a new OC-12 was offered utilizing a Hercules six-cylinder engine and weighing about 12,000lb. The gasoline version had a displacement of 339ci, while the displacement of the diesel was 298ci. Both versions were in the 40 drawbar horsepower class.

A new OC-4 was available in 1956 in either gas or diesel versions using a Hercules three-cylinder engine of 130ci. It

Next page
Oliver "Cletrac" Model OC-3
The Oliver "Cletrac" Model OC-3 used a Hercules engine of 123ci rated at 1700rpm.

was a 5,000lb tractor in the 20 drawbar horsepower class. Finally, rounding out the line, the OC-15, introduced also in 1956, was a 20,000lb tractor in the 70 drawbar horsepower category. It used a six-cylinder Hercules engine of 529ci.

Strangely, in 1960, the White Motor Corporation of Cleveland, Ohio, the originator of the Cletrac, bought The Oliver Corporation. Within three years, the new owners had discontinued crawler production, ending Cletrac's glorious forty-seven-year history.

Previous page
1960 Minneapolis-Moline MoTrac
M-M master collector Roger Mohr of Vail, Iowa, owns this rare and unusual 1960 MoTrac Mopower crawler excavator. It is powered by the same engine as the M-M Four Star wheel tractor. A five-speed transmission is used with a shuttle control.

1960 Minneapolis-Moline MoTrac
Minneapolis-Moline first came out with its crawler in 1958, and it was to be known as the "Gold Cat." For reasons that will be obvious to some, they had trademark trouble with that name. Next, they called it the "Two Star," following a number-star format that had been set up for their wheel tractors. In fact, the sheet metal and grill for the crawler were the same as that for the Four Star wheel tractor. Finally, in late 1959, the name MoTrac was adopted. This one is owned by Roger Mohr of Vail, Iowa.

1960 Minneapolis-Moline MoTrac
The instrument panel and controls of Roger Mohr's MoTrac crawler excavator. The curved levers with rubber hand grips are the steering controls. Each lever controls first a clutch and then a brake for its corresponding track. The MoTrac was available in either gasoline or diesel versions. Fewer than 250 MoTracs were built, about two-thirds of which were diesel.

Chapter 5

Monarch and Allis-Chalmers

*By means of the track distribution of weight is effected over an area of ground the
equal of which is not covered under any other than this track laying principle of construction.*
—Victor Pagé,
The Modern Gas Tractor: Its Construction, Operation, Application and Repair, 1917

The Monarch Tractor Company

Monarch began building crawler tractors in 1913 in Watertown, Wisconsin. The unique feature of the Monarch line was the dual teeth on the drive and idler sprockets. This feature kept the tracks from coming off in turns or on side hills. Three sizes were built in this period: the Lightfoot 6-10, the Neverslip 12-20, and the Neverslip 18-30.

The Lightfoot 6-10 was an inexpensive lightweight, 3,000lb machine aimed at the family farmer. Besides the dual sprocket teeth feature, the Lightfoot had overlapping, staggered bogie wheels. Power came from a four-cylinder Kermath engine.

The Neverslip 12-20 featured an angle-iron track frame with inverted T-beams to hold the bogies. The four-cylinder Erd engine was mounted crosswise.

The Model 18-30 had track frames like the Neverslip, but with a cast-iron loop in front tying the inner and outer frames together. The 18-30 used a longi-

tudinally mounted Beaver four-cylinder engine. The output end of the engine was forward, however, with the clutch, gearbox, and differential at the front. Chain drives were used to reach the rear drive sprockets. The 18-30 was redesigned in 1921 and redesignated the 20-30. The new version used a three-speed, rather than a two-speed transmission.

Each of the three Monarch tractors of this period used a steering wheel for

1939 Allis-Chalmers Model S

The S was a large Allis-Chalmers crawler weighing in at over 20,000lb and employing a 675ci engine. This 1939 model is owned and driven by Norm Meinert of Davis, Illinois. Meinert is one of the organizers of the Freeport (Illinois) Show, and is an officer in the Stephenson County Antique Engine Club.

1934 Allis-Chalmers Model K

This Allis-Chalmers Model K was seen at the 1992 Thresherman's Reunion in Pontiac, Illinois. The Model K was originally produced as the Monarch 35 before Monarch was acquired by Allis-Chalmers in 1928. Production continued through 1943. The Model K was powered by a four-cylinder Allis-Chalmers gasoline engine of 461ci. An orchard version was also available. For it, the operator's seat and controls were moved back and down and protrusions above the hood were minimized.

1936 Allis-Chalmers Model L
The size of the Model L Allis-Chalmers dwarfs its operator, owner Norm Meinert of Davis, Illinois. This 22,000lb Model L is powered by a six-cylinder Allis-Chalmers engine of 844ci. Maximum brake horsepower produced during the Nebraska Tests was 91.93. The Model L was produced from 1931 through 1942; this one is a 1936 model.

control, rather than levers. The wheel controlled an externally contracting brake on either side of the differential.

The Monarch Tractor Company reorganized in 1919 as Monarch Tractors, Incorporated. Manufacturing facilities remained in Watertown, Wisconsin,

with additional plants in Brantford, Ontario, Passaic, New Jersey, and Berlin, Wisconsin.

The next Monarch was the Model D-6-60, first offered in 1924. In appearance, the Model D was similar to the previous Monarchs, with the frame loop around the front of the tracks. The Model D had a 60hp six-cylinder Beaver engine, however, making it much more powerful than any of its predecessors. This 17,000lb tractor had a maximum drawbar pull of almost 13,000lb. The Monarch D was normally equipped with a cab.

The Monarch Model C followed the D in late 1924. The C was powered by a

Next page
1936 Allis-Chalmers Model L
This 1936 L crawler had dual carburetors and dual exhausts. The 844ci engine develops about 90hp at 1050rpm. It can easily go through its 75 gallon fuel supply in a day's work. The source of the "live hydraulics" is protruding from under the radiator. Norm Meinert bought this tractor in Monroe, Wisconsin.

four-cylinder Beaver engine. It was much the same configuration as the old 18-30, but was now rated as a 25-35. It weighed a little over 5 tons. The Monarch Model E was an industrial version of this tractor.

1939 Allis-Chalmers Model S
Norm Meinert of Davis, Illinois, is an inveterate Allis-Chalmers collector and restorer. Norm bought this 1939 S on sealed bids from a township highway department. The crawler, fitted with a factory cab, was used in opening drifted rural roads with a Vee snowplow.

Financial troubles continued to dog the Monarch outfit, and it was again reorganized in the Spring of 1925 as the Monarch Tractor Corporation of Springfield, Illinois. Two tractors were introduced by the new company, the 10-Ton Model F and the 6-Ton Model H. The Model F used a 6.50x7.00in bore and stroke Beaver LeRoi four-cylinder engine, while the 6-Ton Model H used a Sterns four-cylinder engine of 5.12x 6.50in bore and stroke.

Allis-Chalmers Manufacturing Company

The roots of Allis-Chalmers go all the way back to 1842 when the first of its ancestor companies (the Gates Iron Works) was founded. It was 1901, however, before the Allis-Chalmers Company was formed. The company was named for Milwaukee industrialist Edwin P. Allis and Chicago manufacturer William J. Chalmers whose holdings were merged. The company was located in Milwaukee, Wisconsin. It was a large producer of steam powerplants, sawmills, and mining equipment.

By 1913, the company had overextended itself and had gone into receivership. The receivers reorganized the company as the Allis-Chalmers Mfg. Co. (the abbreviations being the official spelling). General Otto H. Falk (Wisconsin National Guard, retired), was appointed president. Falk brought Allis-Chalmers into the tractor business the

next year. From then until his retirement in 1932, tractors were a pet project for General Falk. Harry Merritt was appointed by General Falk to manage the tractor activities, and it was Merritt who decided in 1929 to paint Allis-Chalmers tractors Persian Orange; until that time, tractors were always painted in dull colors such as gray or green.

In 1928, the Monarch Tractor Company was added to Allis-Chalmers. The Monarch Models F and H were in production at the time Monarch was acquired by Allis-Chalmers, and they were redesignated the Model 75 and 50, respectively. The Monarch name was retained for a few years.

In 1932, the engine of the Model 50 was changed to an Allis-Chalmers four-cylinder engine of 5.25x6.50in bore and stroke. The displacement of the LeRoi engine in the Model 75 was increased by enlarging the bore from 6.50 to 6.75in, giving it a respectable displacement of 1002ci.

The first crawler to be distinctively "A-C" was the Model 35, brought out in 1929. It was not available with a belt pulley, so belt ratings were not tested during the Nebraska Tests done in November 1929. A rear PTO was offered, however, as combines and balers requiring PTO power were quite popular by then. The 35 was powered by a four-cylinder Allis-Chalmers gasoline engine of 461ci. An orchard version of the 35 was available. For it, the operator's seat and controls were moved back and down and protrusions above the hood were minimized.

The 35 was later called the Model K, and the Monarch name was dropped. It was at this time that the steering wheel was dropped in favor of steering levers. This was the case for all subsequent Allis-Chalmers crawlers.

During 1935, a K-O model was produced; the "O" standing for "oil," as an oil engine was used, which was a semi-diesel. Fuel injectors were used, but compression was not high enough for

1941 Allis-Chalmers Model WM

The Allis-Chalmers Model M was introduced in 1932 and produced through 1942. It shared its engine with the Allis-Chalmers Model U wheel tractor. The engine was the 4.37x5.0in bore and stroke UM engine. The Model M crawler had a rated brake horsepower of 32.01 and weighed about 6,600lb. In 1937, the UM engine displacement was increased by enlarging the bore to 4.50in. Over 14,000 Allis Ms were made. Some, like the 1941 model shown, were WMs, or wide-gauge models. This one is owned by Alan Draper, an English collector/restorer. The tractor is shown plowing at the Great Dorset Steam Fair with Alan at the controls. The annual Great Dorset Steam Fair encompasses about three times the area shown in this photo, with thousands of tractors, trucks, and steam engines on either static or active display.

auto-ignition. Therefore, a magneto and spark plugs set off the charge. There were also K-W and K-O-W versions, the "W" indicating wide tracks. Production of the Model K continued to 1943.

1934 Allis-Chalmers Model K
Originally built by Monarch Tractors as the 35, it was called the Model K after Allis-Chalmers took over in 1934. Soon after the steering wheel was replaced with steering levers. During 1935, a K-O model was produced; the "O" standing for "oil," as a semi-diesel oil engine was used.

The next purely Allis-Chalmers crawler was the Model L (probably standing for "Large"). This 22,000lb monster was powered first by a six-cylinder Continental engine, but this was soon replaced by a six-cylinder Allis-Chalmers engine of 844ci. Maximum

brake horsepower produced during the Nebraska Tests was 91.93. The Model L replaced the Model 75 in 1932. Production continued through 1942. A few, possibly twenty, Model L-O (oil engine) tractors were built in 1935.

The Allis-Chalmers Model M was announced in 1932. It had the distinction of sharing its engine with the famous Allis-Chalmers Model U wheel tractor. The engine, was the 4.37x5.00in bore and stroke UM engine. The Model M crawler had a rated brake horsepower of 32.01 as determined by the Nebraska Tests. The tractor weighed 6,620lb for the tests. In 1937, the UM engine's displacement was increased by enlarging

the bore to 4.50in. It is noteworthy that there were several crawler conversions of the Model U wheel tractor. Thus equipped, the Model U had the distinction of offering one of, if not the first, hydraulically operated bulldozer blades.

The final offering by Allis-Chalmers in the pre-1940 arena was the Model S. The S was another large crawler weighing in at over 20,000lb and employing a 675ci engine. There was also a Model S-O oil engine version.

Allis Chalmers saw the light in 1940 and dropped the oil engine. In its place was the General Motors two-cycle supercharged diesel. The engine was a modular design based on a 71ci cylinder. Any

number of cylinders could be specified in order to get the desired power. The engine is still in routine use at this writing in applications from trucks to ships.

Being a two-cycle, the GM has combustion every time the piston comes up. This makes it sound like it is turning twice as fast as a comparable four-cycle engine. The high-speed firing, coupled with the howl of the blower makes a GM two-cycle diesel sound like an ungoverned four-cycle engine in neutral with the throttle wide open. Despite the fact that they sound like they are about to blow, the GM diesel is a long-life, thrifty powerplant.

Allis-Chalmers' first application of the GM diesel was in its new HD-14. It used six of the 71ci cylinders, and the engine was called a GM 6-71. The 426ci total displacement, and a rated engine speed of 1500rpm, made the HD-14 the most powerful crawler of its time. Significantly, it was able to pull 97 percent of its own weight in the Nebraska drawbar pull test: the tractor weighed

28,750lb, and it pulled 28,019lb. Remarkably, the HD-14 recorded a rated-load fuel consumption of 15.18hp hours per gallon of diesel fuel. By comparison, the A-C L-O recorded 9.77hp hours per gallon; even the highly touted Caterpillar D7, which was tested just before the HD-14, produced only 14.81hp hours per gallon. The HD-14 demonstrated a maximum load brake horsepower of 145.39.

The next Allis-Chalmers diesel was the HD-10. This unit used a GM 4-71 engine. At its rated 1600rpm, the HD-10 delivered 86hp and 14hp hours per gallon. The HD-10 weighed 21,630lb. Finally, in the new series for 1940, was the HD-7. This was a 14,000lb tractor using a GM 3-71 engine of 60 brake horsepower at 1500rpm.

Allis-Chalmers continued some of its gasoline tractors into the decade, as well as the new diesels. Other GM-powered diesels, with the 71ci cylinder, were added as time went on, such as the giant HD-19 of 1947, and the HD-15 and HD-9 of 1951. Also in 1951, the HD-20

1934 Allis-Chalmers Model K
There were also K-W and K-O-W versions. The "W" indicated wide-gage tracks. Production of the Model K continued to 1943. Alan Draper owns this 1934 model.

was introduced with a GM 6-110 (110ci per cylinder) engine. This was a massive 42,625lb tractor that found little use in agriculture. It was probably tested at the University of Nebraska just to impress the test engineers. In fact, belt tests could not be done because of limited capability of the dynamometer.

By 1955, Allis-Chalmers had readied its own series of diesel engines, and discontinued the use of the "Howling Jimmy." The new Allis-Chalmers engines were first used in the HD-21. It was an 844ci six-cylinder supercharged engine. This engine was also used in the HD-16, but without the supercharger. The next year, the HD-6 and HD-11 came out with Allis-Chalmers engines. These models carried the company banner into 1960.

Chapter 6

International Harvester Company

The ordinary wheel with a 24-inch base width in order to cover an area equal to that of one 24-inch track would have to be 120 feet in diameter and would weigh more than fifteen tons. Obviously, this is not a practical construction.
—Victor Pagé,
The Modern Gas Tractor: Its Construction, Operation, Application and Repair, 1917

Cyrus McCormick and William Deering were principle pioneers in the farm implement business. McCormick founded his company in 1840, following his invention of the reaper.

A latecomer in the crawler field, IHC produced its first crawler in 1929. It was essentially a McCormick-Deering 10-20 wheel tractor converted to tracks. International Harvester's name for it was the TracTracTor. A TracTracTor based on the 15-30 wheel tractor was also made available about the same time. A T-20 TracTracTor was made available in 1932. It was based on the powertrain of the Farmall F-20, which included a 221ci kerosene-burning engine. The T-20 continued in production until 1940.

Early TracTracTors had an unusual steering clutch arrangement. A pair of co-axial "tower" shafts (one for each track) came up through the floor of the cockpit. On top of each was a dome-shaped housing containing the steering

1932 McCormick-Deering T-40 TracTracTor
The T-40 appeared in 1932 and was produced through 1939. It used a six-cylinder engine of 279ci, the same as that of the W-40 wheel tractor. Ike Martyn of Edgar, Wisconsin, restored this machine from a basket of parts. The engine and tracks came from another tractor. New sprockets were obtained. Ike Martyn bought this T-40 in the Junction City, Wisconsin, area.

clutch. Steering levers extended from each of these domes. A pair of steering brake pedals were located on the floor on the right side. A master clutch pedal was on the left. For most of the T-20 TracTracTors, the steering clutches were below the floor in a conventional manner.

An upsized model called the T40 appeared in 1932 and was produced through 1939. It used a six-cylinder engine of 279ci the same as that of the W-40 wheel tractor. Rated brake horsepower was 43.33. The T-40 weighed 10,790lb for its Nebraska Test in October 1932.

In 1934, International Harvester's first diesel tractor came out: a version of the T-40 called the TD-40. It was powered by a 461ci four-cylinder overhead-valve engine capable of 48hp. The new IH diesel was started on gasoline, with a carburetor, spark plugs, and a magneto ignition system provided. When the engine was running on gasoline, a lever was thrown closing off the gasoline combustion chambers and engaging the fuel injectors. Then the engine continued running on diesel fuel. Fuel consumption was about half that of the gasoline T-40.

The next International Harvester crawler, the T-35, came out in 1936. Production did not really get underway until the next year, however. The T-35 was like a scaled-up T-20. Its engine was the same as the original T-40. The six-cylin-

der unit of 279ci was available in either distillate or gasoline versions. The distillate version was rated at 37hp and the gasoline version at 40hp. The T-35 weighed about 10,500lb. It continued in production until 1939. A diesel version, the TD-35, was also offered with a 413ci four-cylinder engine.

By 1937, the displacement of the T-40 engine had been increased above that of the T-35. The T-40 gasoline and distillate engines displaced 298ci while the diesel T-40 stayed at 461ci.

International Harvester got into truly heavyweight crawlers in late 1938 when the TD-18 was introduced. It was the first of the line of striking red tractors with smooth sheet metal contours and purposeful grilles, both crawler and wheel, designed by the famous industrial designer, Raymond Loewy. The TD-18 was a 23,000lb class crawler. Its engine had the same bore and stroke as that of the TD-40, but six cylinders were used instead of four. The TD-18 demonstrated a drawbar pull of 18,973lb during its testing at Nebraska in March 1939.

IHC offered a line of crawlers as it went into the decade of the 1940s. The T-6 model had the same 248ci engine and five-speed transmission as the Farmall M, and was considered a three-to-four plow machine. It was available, at least early on, in both gasoline and distillate versions. The TD-6 had the same

1936 McCormick-Deering T-20 TracTracTor
The T-20 TracTracTor was first built in 1932. It was based on the powertrain of the Farmall F-20, which included a 221ci kerosene-burning engine. The T-20 continued in production until 1940. The 1936 model shown is owned by Ike Martyn of Edgar, Wisconsin. He and his sons repinned the tracks, but the sprockets were shot. When obtaining replacements proved impossible, Ike took the best of the two to Hartford Manufacturing, where he worked. Using a Photocell copying cutter, he had two new sprockets made at once by copying the old one.

1936 McCormick-Deering T-20 TracTracTor
The unique track tensioning mechanism of the T-20 is shown here. This tractor is owned by Ike Martyn of Edgar, Wisconsin. It spent most of it's life in pulping in the Mosinee, Wisconsin, area.

transmission and chassis, but used the 248ci diesel engine from the Farmall MD. The T-6 weighed about 7,700lb, while the TD-6 weighed about 8,000lb.

The next step up in size for an IHC crawler was the T-9/TD-9. It offered about 15 more horsepower than the T-6, and weighed in at almost 11,000lb. It was rated for five to seven 14in plows. The four-cylinder engine had a counterpart in W-9/WD-9 wheel tractors, and was available in gasoline or diesel versions only. By 1960, the TD-9 had grown to 14,000lb and had a six-cylinder 282ci turbocharged engine of 70hp.

The T-14/TD-14, introduced in 1939, was continued through 1949 (the T-14 was dropped in 1946). It was IHC's most popular crawler, and the largest used routinely for farm work. In 1949, an improved TD-14A came out. Improve-

ments in the 461ci engine resulted in a maximum belt horsepower of 72. The TD-14A weighed about 15,000lb.

In 1947, International Harvester began production of the giant TD-24 crawler. It weighed almost 41,000lb. Its six-cylinder engine displaced 1091ci. The transmission featured eight forward speeds. During its Nebraska Test in 1950, the TD-24 pulled 4,892lb in eighth gear at 8mph.

A new TD-18 came out in 1955, offering a 691ci six-cylinder engine. It weighed about 30,000lb. The transmission had six forward speeds.

The TD-15 was tested at the University of Nebraska in July of 1960. A 554ci six-cylinder engine provided a maximum drawbar horsepower of 77. The TD-15 was a 25,000lb tractor.

A break in the TD designation scheme came with the T-340. The T-340 was a crawler version of the Farmall and International 340 models. The engine was the gasoline C-135 unit of 4.25x 4.13in bore and stroke. The T-340 weighed just under 7,000lb. It reflected the new (in 1958) styling for IHC farm

The success of the T-340 prompted International Harvester to come out with three new models for the farm in 1960. All had ample clearance for crops, a five-speed transmission with the optional Torque Amplifier, optional three-point hitch, live PTO, and a choice of track gauges and shoe widths.

First was the T-4, using the 122.7ci four-cylinder engine of the Farmall 140 and 240 wheel tractors. The T-4 weighed just under 7,000lb. Next, the T-5, weighing just over 7,000lb, used the 135ci engine. Lastly, the TD-5 arrived. This was a diesel version with a 144ci engine. It

McCormick-Deering TD-40 Diesel TracTracTor

In 1934, International Harvester's first diesel tractor came out: a version of the T-40 called the TD-40. It was powered by a 461ci four-cylinder overhead-valve engine capable of 48hp. The new IH diesel was started on gasoline; with a carburetor, spark plugs, and a magneto ignition system provided. Fuel consumption was about half that of the gasoline T-40. International Harvester tractors were gray until 1936, thereafter they were red, as is the T-40 shown here.

Previous page
1936 McCormick-Deering T-20 TracTracTor
Early TracTracTors, such as the one shown, had an unusual steering clutch arrangement. A pair of co-axial "tower" shafts (one for each track) came up through the floor of the cockpit. On top of each was a dome-shaped housing containing the steering clutch. Steering levers extended from each of these domes. A pair of steering brake pedals were located on the floor on the right side.

tractors. In 1960, a Model TD-340 was introduced. It featured a 166ci diesel engine.

McCormick-Deering T-40 TracTracTor

The T-40 used a six-cylinder 3.75x4.50in engine, identical to the W-40 wheel-type tractors. It had seven main bearings, forced-feed lubrication, and replaceable cylinder liners. It burned about 6 gallons per hour at maximum load. More than 1,600 T-40s were built between 1932 and 1939. Selling price averaged about $2,800.

weighed about 7,200lb. These three crawlers were rated at 26.3, 30.9, and 28.5 drawbar horsepower, respectively. Finally, rounding out the 1940–1960 time frame, the 52,000lb TD-25, providing 185 drawbar horsepower. The 817ci six-cylinder engine was turbocharged.

International Harvester T-4, T-5, and TD-5 Brochure

IHC's crawler lineup featured the T-4 with 26.3 drawbar horsepower, the T-5 with 30.9hp, and the diesel TD-5 with 28.5hp.

International Harvester T-6
This T-6 International Harvester crawler was just right for many farm uses. The T-6 had the same 248ci engine and five-speed transmission as the Farmall M, and was considered a three- to four-plow machine. It was originally available in both gasoline and distillate versions; later, the distillate was dropped in favor of a diesel, called the TD-6. The photo was taken at the 1993 Sycamore Show, near Sycamore, Illinois.

Chapter 7

Deere & Company

For use wherever extra flotation is needed...in light soils, wet, loose ground, rough terrain, woodlands, etc. For use wherever extra stability, such as on extreme hillsides, is essential.
—Deere & Company Model MC brochure

John Deere was another latecomer to the crawler field. In fact, during the era of 1920–1940, John Deere crawlers were really conversions, much as the first IHC TracTracTors were little more than wheel tractors converted into crawlers. In the case of John Deere, the conversions were done by another company: the Lindeman Company of Yakima, Washington.

Jesse Lindeman and his brother, Harry, got into the farm implement business in 1923 by buying the stock of a bankrupt dealer, for which Jesse had worked. Things were going well, so in the next year, the brothers took on a Holt-Caterpillar dealership. This arrangement lasted until 1925, when Holt and Best merged to become the Caterpillar Tractor Company. In the shaking out of Best and Holt dealerships, the Lindemans lost, and the area Best dealer got the job for the new Caterpillar agency.

Not to be thwarted, the Lindemans took on Cletrac. In 1930, as the grip of the Depression tightened, they also ac-

quired a John Deere dealership, which catered to the apple grower in Washington state. Neither the Cletrac, nor the two John Deere models, the D and the GP, were well suited for orchard work, however. They were all too high to fit under the branches and had too many upward protrusions. Lindeman did begin to manufacture some cultivation tools that had extension drawbars, so that they would run out to the side of the tractor and better get close to the tree trunk.

Next, the Lindeman Brothers took a standard-tread GP and modified it with

1945 John Deere BO Lindeman Crawler
The Model BO Lindeman Crawler was built for orchard work in the West. The tractor, less running gear, was sent by John Deere to Lindeman's Yakima, Washington, plant, where tracks were installed.

John Deere D Lindeman Crawler
In 1932, the Lindeman Brothers of Yakima, Washington, modified three John Deere Model D wheel tractors by installing tracks from Best Crawlers. One was shipped to Deere for testing. Because the D was a standard-tread tractor, it was quite low to the ground. Therefore, Deere decided its Model GP tractor, which had more crop clearance, would be better. Further crawler development was then applied to the GP. The D Crawler shown in this photo is hauling an irrigation land leveler. Power was supplied by a two-cylinder engine of 501ci operating at 900rpm. It was capable of 42 belt horsepower. *Deere & Company*

John Deere GPO Lindeman Crawler
The GPO was the Orchard version of the John Deere Model GP tractor. About twenty-five were converted by the Lindeman Brothers of Yakima, Washington, to crawlers. This one is shown with its almost full fender removed to show track details. This is a fairly early GPO with a 312ci two-cylinder engine. It had a maximum belt horsepower of 20. *Deere & Company*

special axle castings to lower it. They also lowered the seat and cleaned up the things sticking out of the hood. The folks at Deere were impressed. The Lindeman's ideas were adopted and John Deere's first orchard tractor was born, the GPO.

In 1932, the brothers again notified John Deere that they had something to show the firm. The Lindemans had installed the tracks from a Best Thirty on a John Deere D. They eventually constructed three of these conversions, which were thoroughly tested by both Lindeman and Deere. The outcome was the decision to drop the tracklayer idea for the D, but to apply it to the GPO.

Lindeman purchased partially finished orchard tractors from Deere and installed a conventional crawler running gear. The tractor featured Deere's side-valve horizontal side-by-side two-cylinder engine. The crawler version weighed about 5,500lb and was in the 15-25hp class. It used a three-speed transmission and originally used differential steering brakes; later, steering clutches were added to improve control.

Deere soon announced that the GP was being replaced by the Model B, and an orchard version of the standard-tread B, the BO, would be offered. The Lindemans immediately began adding tracks.

The Lindeman Crawlers, as they came to be known, were just right for the hilly apple orchards in Washington and

Oregon. The low stance, freedom from protrusions above the hood, and the hillside stability made the Lindemans a good seller. They also found good usage in flat land farming in the West. Because of its Western usage, however, they were never tested at the University of Nebraska.

In 1946, Deere informed Lindeman that the BO/BR model, from which Lindeman-John Deere crawlers were made, would be discontinued. A new model to be introduced in 1947 to counter the Ford-Ferguson N Series utility tractors was to be offered instead to Lindeman for conversion to tracks: the new M Series.

Before 1946 was out, however, Deere & Company bought out the Lindeman Power Equipment Company of Yakima, Washington. Operations at Lindeman continued as before the buyout, with Jesse G. Lindeman being retained to assist with the conversion of the Model M to become the Model MC crawler.

John Deere BO Lindeman Crawler
The only Deere Lindeman to see much production, the BO Crawler was based on the Orchard version of the John Deere Model B. Tractors, less wheels, were shipped to Lindeman in Yakima, Washington, for the addition of the crawler running gear. Some 1,700 of these nifty little machines were made. The one shown in the photo is pulling a beet harvester. Note the 1941 Dodge one-and-a-half-ton truck. *Deere & Company*

1945 John Deere BO Lindeman Crawler
A frail and failing 92-year-old Jesse Lindeman visited the Washington State Pioneer Power Show in August of 1992. The purpose of his trip was the John Deere Lindeman Crawler in this photo. Crawler owner, Harold Schultz, shown in the driver's seat, transported the impeccably restored Model BO Lindeman 2,000 miles from Ollie, Iowa, to Union Gap, Washington, just to show it to its inventor, Jesse Lindeman. Sadly, Jesse Lindeman died less than two months later.

The first John Deere MC crawler emerged from what was now Deere's Yakima Works for the 1949 model year. Looking much less like a conversion, the new MC weighed about 4,000lb and had eye-pleasing styled sheet metal. The engine was the 100.5ci vertical two-cylinder unit developed for the Model M wheel tractor. Turning at a high speed (for John Deere) of 1650rpm, the engine produced a maximum of 22hp. The MC had a three-roller undercarriage with a choice of 10, 12, or 14in tracks. It could be equipped with Deere's version of the three-point hitch that was made famous by the Ford-Ferguson (many would say the Ford-Ferguson was made famous by the three-point hitch).

In 1953, John Deere offered a completely revised line of tractors with new styling, new powerplants, and new operator conveniences. The Model M wheel tractor was replaced by the new Model 40; accordingly, a new crawler, the 40C also appeared. It offered the same improvements in power, operator comfort, and styling as its wheeled counterpart. The weight of the 40C was about the same at 4,000lb. Engine power was increased to 24hp through breathing improvements and raising the engine speed to 1850rpm while retaining 100.5ci.

The 40C had a much improved track system, with a choice of either four or five rollers. The MC, with only three rollers, left much to be desired in durability, traction, and stability, especially when using a bulldozer blade. Most 40Cs came with a heavy perforated metal radiator shield, a necessary feature for logging and forestry.

In 1954, Deere moved the crawler operations, and many of the Yakima employees, to Dubuque, Iowa. Dubuque was the source of the tractors upon which the crawler was based, and it no longer made sense to ship the partially completed tractors to Yakima for finishing.

The year 1956 saw another round of improvements in John Deere tractors and a new three-number designation scheme. The 40C was replaced by the

1945 John Deere BO Lindeman Crawler
John Deere BO (Orchard) tractors were converted to crawler tracks by the Lindeman Brothers of Yakima, Washington. Lindeman Crawlers, as they came to be known, were just right for the hilly apple orchards in Washington and Oregon.

1945 John Deere BO Lindeman Crawler
This is one of between 300 and 400 John Deere BO Lindeman Crawlers still in existence. It is owned by Harold Schultz of Ollie, Iowa. Lindeman also converted a few John Deere Model GPOs and several Ds, a few BRs and one BI. Lindemans are highly prized by John Deere collectors.

1945 John Deere BO Lindeman Crawler
Some clever angles are incorporated into the various levers for controlling the John Deere BO Lindeman to avoid interference.

new Model 420C. Engine displacement was increased by increasing the bore 0.25in, resulting in 113.5ci. Maximum power was now 30hp, making the 420C quite a good performer. Four or five rollers were optional, as was a distillate-burning engine.

The 420C was replaced by the 430C in 1958. It had a new slanted instrument panel and a more comfortable seat. Also available were a direction-reverser transmission and an LPG engine and fuel system.

In 1959 and 1960, four industrial models were introduced. Two of these were wheel tractors and two were crawlers. The crawlers were basically the same as the 430C but including sturdier sheet metal and grille. One of the crawlers, called the 440IC, had the same 113.5ci as the Model 430C except it was rated at 2000rpm. The other, the 440ICD used the GM two-cycle two-cylinder supercharged diesel. The diesel displaced 106ci and turned at 1850rpm. The diesel version produced a maximum of 33hp; the gasoline version was capable of 32hp. The weight of either of the 440C versions was about 7,000lb.

By 1960, the John Deere crawler was a mature machine that was much in demand in construction, farming, and logging. The engines, transmissions, and running gear were capable and reliable. Steering clutches and brakes were controlled by the hand levers. A foot service brake and foot master clutch were used.

CASE

310

AGRICULTURAL CRAWLER

Chapter 8

J. I. Case and American Tractor TeraTrac

*The distribution of the weight over such a great surface eliminates the possibility of the engine
becoming mired where the ground is wet and soft and the tractor cannot pack the
soil and injure its fertility as much as other forms which concentrate a greater amount of
weight on a lesser bearing surface.*
—Victor Pagé,
The Modern Gas Tractor: Its Construction, Operation, Application and Repair, 1917

Although Case had taken a brief excursion into the crawler world with its Model CD back in the 1930s, it was a newcomer to the field in the late 1950s.

The J. I. Case Company, always an innovator, had been established in Racine, Wisconsin, in 1844 by Jerome Increase Case. J. I. Case was born in Oswego, New York, on December 11, 1819. He was the son of Caleb Case, a farmer, and Deborah Jackson Case, a member of the family that included President Andrew Jackson.

Caleb Case bought one of the first groundhog threshing machines when Jerome was just a lad. Naturally, young Jerome assisted his father with its operation. The long hours gave him ample time to consider its limitations. It also became apparent to young Jerome that the future of grain harvesting was not in the lake area of New York, but in the Upper Mississippi River Valley and in the Great Plains of the MidWest. Case, then 22 years old, sensed his opportunity. On credit, he bought six Pitts groundhog

Case 310

The Case 310 Agricultural Crawler was an update of the American Teratrac 300. The engine was a 148ci Case four-cylinder gasoline type with coil ignition and an updraft carburetor. Advertised drawbar horsepower was 30 and belt horsepower was 36. A three-speed transmission was used.

threshers, and started west by rail for a frontier town called Chicago.

During the harvest of 1842, Case sold five of the six groundhogs, retaining one for custom threshing. He finally located himself in the town of Rochester, in the territory of Wisconsin, not far from the town of Racine.

During the winter of 1842–1843, Case built himself a threshing machine along the groundhog line, but with improvements. Case was pleased with the performance of his machine during the harvest of 1843. With that, Case rented a shop in Racine for the purpose of manufacturing threshers for the next season. Thus was the company founded in Racine, where it still is today as part of the agricultural giant, Case-International.

Although Case died in 1891, The J. I. Case Threshing Machine Company, as it was then called, was well established. Having been a farm steam engine maker since 1869, it was only natural for the company to move into the internal-combustion tractor arena. After an abortive attempt in 1892 with a design called the Patterson tractor, Case finally arrived at a viable tractor concept in 1912. What followed was a succession of competitive tractors that built up a loyal following of farmers and construction contractors.

Case weathered good times and bad with aplomb. Like the other major implement companies, however, they

failed to appreciate the significance of the Ford-Ferguson utility tractor, which was unveiled for the press in June 1939. The tractor world has not been the same since.

The feature that made Ford's 9N so special was the hydraulic three-point hitch, brought in by agreement with Harry Ferguson of Ireland. With the Ferguson hitch and custom implements, the 2,500lb, $600 Ford-Ferguson 9N could out-perform tractors weighing and costing twice as much. The Ford-Ferguson also established the trend away from the row-crop configuration and toward the high-axle wide-front, or "utility," configuration.

The oncoming of World War II blurred the competitive image in the tractor business. By the time other tractor makers were reacting to the squat, compact Ford in 1953, it was already on its third iteration and selling at a rate close to 100,000 units per year.

It was at this point that one Marc Rojtman entered the Case picture. Rojtman was a German Jewish refugee from Nazi persecution. His family had been industrialists in the old country, and it wasn't long before Rojtman had established himself in Indiana where he began experimenting with crawler tractors. In 1949, he was able to gain control of the American Steel Dredge Company of Churubusco, Indiana. From that plant, in

Case Model CD
The beautiful Case Model CD from the 1930s was little more than a Model C Industrial with tracks supplied by Trackson. The Trackson Company of Milwaukee, Wisconsin, made track assemblies for most of the popular wheel tractors of the time. First of the conversions was the ubiquitous Fordson, from which the company derived its name. The Model C Case was rated at 17 drawbar and 27 belt horsepower. This picture was taken at the 1993 Sycamore, Illinois, thresheree.

1950, came a line of crawler tractors under the trademark "TeraTrac." The tractor-producing firm was called the American Tractor Company.

It was in late 1956 that the Case board of directors concluded a merger agreement with American Tractor. The agreement included provisions that Marc Rojtman would become general manager of the merged companies. With the new visionary leadership, Case over-

came its general marketing difficulties and has been in the crawler business (albeit not always specifically agricultural crawlers) ever since.

The line of crawlers from American Tractor prior to the merger included three models: the GT-25, GT-30, and the GT-34. The TeraTrac GT-25 was a light, 3,200lb crawler using a 124ci Continental engine of 26hp. A five-roller undercarriage was used. It was the first non-

Ford to use the hydraulic three-point hitch.

The TeraTrac GT-30 came out in 1951 and was continued through 1954. It was basically the same as the GT-25, except it used the Continental 140ci engine. Operating weight of the GT-30 was 4,400lb. It had the distinction of being the first tractor to have a maximum drawbar pull greater than its own weight. It was able to pull 4,518lb during Nebraska Test 471.

The TeraTrac GT-34 was a medium-size crawler using a Continental 162ci engine. It was produced in model years 1951 through 1954. In 1952, a DT-34 diesel version with a Continental 157ci was added.

For 1955 through the time of the merger, the model designation scheme was changed to a three-number series. These were generally picked up by Case on the other side of the merger.

The first of the new Case crawlers was the Model 310. It was a revision of the American 300, which hailed from the TeraTrac GT-30. The Continental engine was replaced by a Case powerplant of 148ci, and a general restyling was accomplished. A Case diesel of the same displacement was added in 1961.

A big Model 800 came out in 1957. It used a 277ci Continental diesel and a torque converter transmission. An updated Model 810 appeared for the 1960 model year. An even larger Model 1010 was also released at that time. It featured a 382ci Continental four-cylinder engine. A smaller version, the Model 610, came out at the same time. It used a 208ci Continental four-cylinder engine.

Chapter 9

Fordson and Ford Conversions

The origins of the Ford Motor Company in 1903 are a part of Americana. What might not be so well understood, however, is the relationship of Henry Ford, its founder, with farming. Although born on a prosperous Michigan farm, young Henry Ford did not take to the job of farming. He would later write, "There was just too much work around the place." As soon as he was old enough, he left for Detroit and a job in industry. The hard manual labor of the farm did, nevertheless, spawn his interest in things mechanical, which might lift from farming some of its burden.

Henry Ford was always tinkering with things mechanical and was often called upon to repair things from watches to steam engines. The Otto-cycle engine held particular fascination for him

and he began experimenting with its design and construction. In 1893, the same year Henry and his wife, Clara, had their only child, Edsel, Henry's first gasoline engine burst into life, clamped to the kitchen sink. By 1896, Ford's "Quadricycle" automobile was a familiar sight on the Detroit streets.

There were to be two failed automotive ventures in Henry Ford's life before the foundation of the Ford Motor Company in 1903. The first was the Detroit Automobile Company; the second was the Henry Ford Company. Finally, with the help of influential investors, the Ford Motor Company was founded. This company had the talent and resources to get into volume production, and by 1906, production was up to 100 cars per day.

Ford and Tractors

It was in 1906 that Ford's interests returned to farming, and he began the first of many tractor experiments. When asked by an interviewer about his tractor interests, he said that his aim was to make farming what it ought to be, the most pleasant and profitable profession in the world. The tractors that resulted from Ford's early experiments left an indelible mark on farming.

Although Ford never produced crawler tractors, tractors from Ford were the most widely used by companies that

1948 Ford 8N with Bombardier Tracks
The half-track kit was a popular aftermarket accessory for Fords and other brands of wheel tractors. This set was manufactured by Bombardier, the Canadian snowmobile and aircraft company. The tractor is a 1948 Ford Model 8N, one of the most widely produced tractors of all time. Although the tracks can be used for field work, they are made for use on snow or mud, such as for cleaning out a cattleyard with the Ford/Dearborn three-point hitch manure loader. This outfit is owned by Palmer Fossum, a well-known Ford collector and parts dealer from Northfield, Minnesota.

1948 Ford 8N with Bombardier Tracks
The lack of a bogey wheel somewhat diminishes the flotation of this track arrangement, but the traction improvement over the wheel tractor is phenomenal—like the difference between two- and four-wheel drive.

Ford 650 with Arps Tracks
Arps half-tracks were much like those from Bombardier, except the Arps used metal links instead of the all-rubber loop of the Bombardier. This 650, with blades front and back, is owned by Palmer Fossum of Northfield, Minnesota. Palmer has a Ford collection that includes at least one of every year model from 1924 through 1960, plus many unusual implements and accessories. Palmer's dog, Shena, is providing escort.

converted wheel tractors to crawlers. The first of these was the Fordson.

The Fordson

The Fordson had its roots in World War I. A Ford engineer named Eugene Farkas had designed a four-wheel, four-cylinder, three-speed machine that featured a worm-drive reduction gear into the differential. It also featured a frameless structure, whereby the engine, transmission, and differential housings acted as the frame of the tractor.

By 1916, the British were engaged in the war, and were becoming concerned about food production, what with the demands of the war for men and horses, and the possibility of disrupted foreign

supply. It was then that the Farkas-designed tractor was demonstrated to the British. The success of these machines in impressing British government officials led to an immediate order for British production. Because he felt he owed something to his roots, Henry Ford agreed to set up a factory in Cork, Ireland.

Because the Ford Motor Company was still a stockholder-owned company, Henry Ford set up a new company to build tractors. Taking his now 23-year-old son, Edsel, in with him, Henry called the new company Henry Ford & Son. Later, in communicating via the transatlantic cable, the name was abbreviated to "Fordson," and that name was used for the tractor when it went into production.

1950 Fordson Major-Roadless Model E TVO
This tractor was called the Fordson Major Roadless Type E, or Model E. Only twenty-five were converted: twelve had Perkins diesels and thirteen had TVO (Tractor Vaporizing Oil) engines. The conversion was done in cooperation with Ford, who supplied the basic machine less wheels. The differential was eliminated in favor of a bevel-gear set. On the axles, clutches and brakes were fitted.

Production was not in Cork, however, until after the war, as resources were in too short supply in Britain. By mid-1918, more than 6,000 little gray Fordsons were farming in Britain, Canada, and the United States.

Fordsons, now designated as the Model F, were produced in the United

1950 Fordson Major-Roadless Model E TVO
The Roadless used a four-roller undercarriage and a high-profile track. This one is owned by S. P. Ridges of Totten, Southampton. It spent its life in the Newbury area doing arable farming. Mr. Ridges bought it in 1973 and restored it over the years.

1952 Fordson-County CFT
This crawler was based on the Fordson Major Diesel. The one shown is a 1952 model, which did general farming work until 1970. The engine was overhauled in 1970, and by 1985, it only had 20 more hours. At this point, it was purchased by its present owner, David Hastings of Billsdon, Leicestershire. David, says it is nice to drive and easy to control.

States and Ireland in great numbers. Production eclipsed that of all the other tractor makers with Ford holding generally 70 percent of the world's market. At its low point in 1922, the price of the Fordson dropped to $395. The Model F weighed about 3,000lbs. Its L-head engine had a displacement of 251ci. It was rated at 10hp on the drawbar and 20hp on the belt.

The Fordson Model F did not have individual wheel brakes—indeed the original Fordsons had no brakes at all, so the earliest conversions to crawlers were to the half-track configuration. The most famous of these was the Trackson, by the Trackson Company of Milwaukee. Another was the Hadfield-Penfield Steel Company's half-track conversion. There were several others, like the Belle City-Johnson Trackpull, and others that eliminated the Fordson's differential and added steering clutches and brakes for a full crawler conversion.

Fordsons were built in Cork and the United States until 1928. Then production transferred to Ford Motor Company, Ltd., of Dagenham, England. At the time of the transfer, the tractor was modernized and called the Fordson Model N. Production of the Model N continued into 1945. The Model N was upgraded to 267ci, which gave it a 23–12hp rating, belt and drawbar. British Fordsons also attracted the attention of conversion companies. The Roadless DG4 was a half-track conversion with the tracks extending aft from the main axle. As with the Trackson and Trackpull conversions, the weight of the Fordson was about doubled (to about 6,000lb) when half-tracks were added.

Following the war years, the Fordson was given another upgrade into the Model E27N configuration. It was now rated at 27hp; later, a 30hp Perkins diesel engine was fitted. Some 23,000

1952 Fordson-County CFT
Made by County Commercial Cars, Ltd., of Fleet, CFT stood for "County Full Track." Standard track shoe width was 12in, but other widths were available.

E27N diesels were delivered by the time production ended in 1952.

The E27N found good use of the Roadless half-track system, as did the Model N. The full-track Roadless conversion was more popular, however. Roadless tracks pioneered the rubber joint, eliminating the high-wear track pins. To improve the balance, the E27N was fitted with a spacer between the engine and gearbox. This tractor was called the Fordson Major Roadless E. Of the twenty-five converted, thirteen had the Perkins diesel. The conversion was done in cooperation with Ford, who supplied the basic machine, less wheels. A bevel gear set was installed in place of the differential, and clutches and brakes were fitted by Roadless.

The most prominent of the Fordson conversions, and probably the nicest, was the County CFT (County Full Track). It was made by County Commercial Cars of Fleet. Starting in 1948, County began converting E27Ns in cooperation with Ford. As with the Roadless, County replaced the differential with a solid drive, and added clutches and brakes. While Roadless used a four-roller undercarriage, County used five rollers. Both County and Roadless used high-profile tracks to get the required ground clearance.

Next came the Fordson New Major, Power Major, and Super Major. These were truly impressive and modern competitive tractors. Eventually, about 90 percent were diesel powered by a Ford-designed engine. Production continued through 1962, when Ford consolidated its worldwide tractor operations. The County Model Z full-crawler conversion, which was much the same as the CFT for the E27N, was applied to this series of Fordsons.

Ford and Ford-Ferguson

Meanwhile, back in the United States, Ford had gotten back in the tractor business. Irishman Harry Ferguson, a charismatic inventor and manufacturer of farm machinery, had invented the three-point implement system with automatic compensation for changing draft loads. Ferguson arranged a demonstration of the tractor he had built with this system, and its integral implements to Henry Ford at Ford's Fair Lane estate. When it out-plowed a Fordson, Henry Ford struck a Gentleman's Agreement with Ferguson on the spot to build a new tractor incorporating the "Ferguson System."

After less than a year of design and development, in June 1939, the new Ford-Ferguson 9N was unveiled for the press. It was a 2,300lb tractor that pioneered the "utility" configuration. It was rated at 23hp on the belt. The tractor was an immediate success with more than 10,000 being sold yet that year. It was given a minor upgrade in 1942 and redesignated the 2N. Then in 1946, with Henry Ford II in control of the Ford Motor Company, Ferguson was told that the Handshake Deal was over.

Ford then began construction of a completely new model (although it looked much the same) called the 8N for introduction in the 1948 model year. Ford also designed and built its own complete line of implements and set up its own dealer network. The 8N began life with the same engine as the 9N and 2N, but its power grew slightly with a compression ratio increase. Production ended in 1952.

The tractors built by Ford were always quite light for their power and were built with a low stance. Because of these two factors, they made good candidates for conversion to crawler tracks. After World War II, two prominent half-track conversions appeared. The first by the Arps Manufacturing Company of New Holstein, Wisconsin, used a metal link track and a rubber-tired mid-wheel. The second was by Bombardier, the Canadian snowmobile and aircraft company. The Bombardier system was much like the Arps, except it used rubber-belted tracks with metal cross-links. The tracks were obviously based on snowmobile track technology.

Chapter 10

Orphan Crawlers

The increased area of contact between the traction members and the ground means better traction and increased drawbar horse-power.
—Victor Pagé,
The Modern Gas Tractor: Its Construction, Operation, Application and Repair, 1917

The Bullock Tractor Company

The Bullock Tractor Company of Chicago, Illinois, rose from the ashes of the Western Implement Company of Davenport, Iowa. Western had produced some fairly good Creeping Grip half-track machines from about 1910 to 1912, ranging from 25 to 75hp.

In 1916, Bullock built an advanced 6,700lb crawler tractor called the Creeping Grip 12-20. It used a Waukesha four-cylinder engine. Drive was after the fashion of the Best machines, in that a differential and brakes were used for steering. The final drive, however, was chain.

In 1919, the Bullock 12-20 model was replaced by a modernized Model 18-30. Shortly thereafter, the company was purchased by the Franklin Tractor Company of Greenville, Ohio. The 18-30 was modified to be the Franklin 15-30. A feature of the new Franklin model was a

Yuba Ball-Tread 12-20

The Yuba track system relied on 2.25in diameter ball bearings, rather than bogie wheels. The balls were so disbursed around the track frame that there was a pair for each track link at all times. This 1916 photo shows the Yuba pulling a three-bottom John Deere plow during a demonstration. From the flying dust and blurred track, it appears to be moving right along.
Deere & Company

front-mounted cable winch, which could be used in construction and logging.

Yuba Manufacturing Company

The problem of side loads on the tracks was addressed in an innovative way by the Ball Tread Company. The Ball Tread Company was formed in 1912 in Detroit, Michigan. Yuba Construction Company of Marysville, California, took over Ball in 1914. Yuba's main interest was in dredging equipment for the Yuba River gold fields. The Yuba Construction Company later became the Yuba Manufacturing Company.

A former C. L. Best shop foreman named C. A. Henneuse invented the innovative track system. It relied on 2.25in diameter ball bearings, rather than bogie wheels. The track frame was actually a pair of parallel ball-bearing raceways. Like raceways were incorporated into the track. Thus, the track rolled around the frame on these balls. Besides providing unequaled dispersal of the footprint pressure, the balls provided the same supporting surface area when the tractor was turning, or when it was operating on a side hill, as on flat ground going straight. The balls were so dispersed that there was a pair for each track link at all times.

Another unique feature of the Ball Tread tractor was its reversing and steer-

ing arrangement. A differential gearbox was used with each track. Brake bands, controlled by the steering levers, could stop one or the other of the differential output members. For straight ahead, one brake band was applied on each track. For reverse, the other band was applied on both tracks. For turning, both bands could be released on one side, or for a more rapid turn, the reverse band could be applied to one side. Control was much like hydrostatic steering and reversing mechanisms of today. Nevertheless, the Ball Tread tractor also used the front tiller wheel.

The original Ball Tread was a 12-25 model, powered by a four-cylinder Continental engine. Later models used Wisconsin and Waukesha engines. Finally in 1919, a huge 21,000lb monster was offered with Yuba's own 1128ci engine. Production of Ball Tread tractors continued until it was ended by the Great Depression in about 1930.

The JT Tractor Company

Not much history remains concerning the JT outfit. It is known that the firm built crawler tractors in Cleveland from 1918 through about 1926, and that they had a relatively good reputation as farm and logging machines.

Two models were built: the 16-30 and 30-45. The 16-30 used a Chief four-cylinder engine and weighed about

Next page
1920 JT Ad
Although not too obvious from these old photos, the JT's belt pulley was at the front of the tractor, driven by a bevel gearbox. This 1920 *Prairie Farmer* magazine ad touts the capability of the JT "on the belt." The belt pulley had cork inserts in the steel wheel for traction.

1920 JT Ad
"Easy riding and steering. Sensitive as a good motor car." Such are the features of the JT crawler lauded in this 1920 *Prairie Farmer* advertisement.

7,000lb. The 30-45 used a four-cylinder Climax KU engine. These engines were of relatively high compression and operated on gasoline, although kerosene versions were available. Both JTs were steered by a T-handle, which controlled differential brakes.

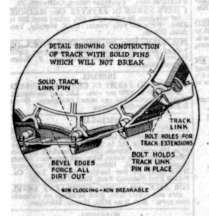

Chapter 11

British Crawlers

"The American Holt Caterpillar has no military significance."
—German military officer, after a 1913 demonstration

The world's first tracklayer to be steered by slowing one or the other track without a tiller wheel was built in Great Britain in 1904 by the Hornsby-Akroyd firm. Hornsby-Akroyd badgered the British military for ten years before giving up the idea of an armored crawler rolling over trenches and barbed wire. Hornsby-Akroyd later sold its crawler track patents to the Holt Company in America.

Before the year 1914 was out, the British military changed its mind. Employees of Holt were sent for to come to England to demonstrate the crawler. The Army also sent Lieutenant Colonel Ernest Swinton, a military man enamored with the possibilities of armored crawlers, to Peoria. The outcome was that thousands of Holts were purchased by the Allied powers to pull artillery to the battlefield. Colonel Swinton went on to see his "armed, armored crawler" become the world's first tank, a machine that turned the war in favor of the Allies.

From the days of World War I, the crawler farm tractor thrived on the soil conditions in the British Isles. The weight-spreading capacity of the track-laying machine allowed tillage and timber harvesting in areas impossible for conventional vehicles. England was also a pioneer in the area of four-wheel-drive tractors, both skid-steer and articulated, because of so much poor footing.

Fowler

Cable plowing was also invented by the English, before the turn of the Twentieth Century. The heavy steam engine stayed on the headland while the plow (plough) shuttled across and back on a cable.

One of the big players in the cable plowing arena was John Fowler. He established his company at Leeds in about 1850. John Fowler died in 1864, but family members kept the firm going into the crawler tractor era.

In 1927, the first Fowler Gyrotiller was built at the Leeds factory. This was a machine developed specifically for sugar cane cultivation, with twin counter-rotating horizontal disks with teeth extending downward. The machine and disks were driven by a 225hp engine, and the disks could be raised and lowered by engine power. When fully lowered, the disks could break soil to a depth of 20in. Needless to say, this was quite a heavy machine. To support its great weight, Fowler (with the help of Holt) built a tracked running gear for it.

The Ricardo engine consumed fuel at the rate of 14 gallons per hour when the disks were at depth, but in that hour an acre could be prepared for seed. When diesel engines became commonly available, the gas-guzzling Ricardo was replaced.

Fowler manufactured Gyrotillers until 1937, and many were exported to the Caribbean sugar plantations.

Following World War II, Fowler merged with Marshall of Gainsborough, which was already building a successful farm wheel tractor. At the time of the merger, Fowler had a new crawler series under development. These were to be called the Challenger, Marks 1, 2 ,3, and 4.

The Mark 3 came first in 1950. It was powered by either a Leyland or a Meadows diesel of 95hp. It weighed about 24,000lb, and featured a five-roller track system.

Next came the Mark 1 in 1951, the smallest of the line. It had an unusual supercharged two-cycle, two-cylinder engine made by Marshall. Interestingly, this model used a Coventry pony motor for starting. The Mark 1 had the distinction of having PTO shafts available at the front, side, and rear.

1950 Fowler-Marshall VF Crawler

Marshall tractors are a familiar sight in Britain and Europe, but are quite rare in America. Based on the Field Marshall wheel tractor, the VF crawler is even more rare. It was made in conjunction with Marshall's stablemate, Fowler. The engine is an impressive 396ci single-cylinder two-cycle diesel. It produces 40hp at 750rpm. A. and L. Carter of Winborne, Dorset, England, own this one.

1930 Fowler Gyrotiller

An early British crawler was the Fowler Gyrotiller. Fowler was a pioneer British steam engine maker. After World War I, the market for steam equipment diminished rapidly. The story told is that C. H. Fowler saw a Gyrotiller, and met its inventor, while vacationing in the Caribbean. Fowler supposedly bought the patent rights on the spot. He hoped the tiller would replace steam engines as a source of revenue. As it turned out, British soil conditions did not always lend themselves to such tillage and most Gyrotillers were exported. Nevertheless, Fowler did develop a good crawler and survived until well into the 1970s.

Fowler Gyrotiller

The Gyrotiller was developed specifically for sugar cane cultivation, with twin counter-rotating horizontal disks with teeth extending downward. When fully lowered, the disks could break soil to a depth of 20in.

A Challenger Mark 2 was built from 1951 to about 1954. It was a scaled-down version of the Mark 3, with a 65hp Leyland diesel engine.

Finally, in 1953, came the big Mark 4. It was powered by a 150hp Meadows diesel and weighed some 15 tons. Somewhat large for British farm duties, most were sold for export.

Challenger production continued until 1974 when Fowler ceased production and dropped from the market.

Marshall

Marshall-built wheel-type farm tractors have been a familiar sight and sound in Great Britain since 1930. It was one of the first, if not the first, diesel farm tractor. The diesel was a single cylinder, two-cycle type, with an ejector-type straight exhaust. If the exhaust note of the two-cylinder John Deere captivated the Americans, the 700rpm Marshall captivated the British with its sound.

Following World War II, the Marshall was updated and fitted with handsome sheet metal to be called the Field Marshall. The 6.50x9.00in bore and stroke one-cylinder diesel engine was speeded up to 750rpm to produce a respectable 40hp. The unique engine was one of the few diesels that could be started by a hand crank. To facilitate starting, a cigarette-like piece of paper was lighted and inserted into a hole provided. The smoldering paper acted like a glow-plug. The crank, a two-hander, came out the side. The concern in starting a Field Marshall was not the possibility of breaking your wrist in a kick-back, but for breaking your legs. For cold weather, Field Marshalls were fitted with a cartridge starter. A shotgun-shell-size cartridge was placed in a chamber and

Fowler Gyrotiller

Fowler built its first Gyrotiller at its Leeds factory in 1927. The machine and its twin sugar cane cultivating disks were driven by a 225hp engine. The disks could be raised and lowered by engine power.

1950 Fowler Challenger Mark 2
A studio photo of the British Fowler Challenger Mark 2, which came out in 1950. It featured a 65hp Leyland diesel engine.

1950 Fowler-Marshall VF Crawler
This crawler is based on the Field Marshall wheel tractor, which was popular in Great Britain in the 1940s and 1950s. The one-cylinder 40hp two-cycle diesel has a 6.50in bore and a 9.00in stroke. Four radiators are used. Starting is by hand crank (inserted into the 2,500lb flywheel just ahead of the top roller), or by explosive cartridge.

fired. After the smoke cleared, the engine should have been running. Cartridges were expensive, so the hand crank was used whenever possible.

In 1947, along with the merger with Fowler, a Series 2 Field Marshall was unveiled. Among its improvements were differential wheel brakes. Hand-in-hand with the Fowler engineers, crawler tracks were fitted to the Series 2 Field Marshall. This model was designated the VF.

The final version of the crawler Field Marshall was the Model VFA. It was based on the Series 3 and 3A wheel tractor. This version had a six-speed gearbox. The 3A type was painted orange, rather than green, and sported a hydraulic three-point lift.

Production of the Field Marshall line came to an end in 1957.

Ransomes
Possibly the oldest of names in the farm equipment business, the firm of Ransomes, Simms and Jefferies, dates back to 1789. The company was a pioneer British tillage tool maker and made the world's first portable farm steam engine. Experiments with internal-combustion tractors dates to around the turn of the Twentieth Century.

Ransomes, which hails from Ipswich, is known for a line of tiny market garden crawlers. The first to be offered commercially was the MG2 of 1936. It was just under 6ft long, 3ft wide, and weighed just over 1,000lb. The engine was the Sturmey-Archer one-cylinder air-cooled 6hp unit.

Two more versions of the Ransomes mini-crawler were produced. The MG-5, came out in 1949, was an updated version of the MG-2. The engine was improved to produce 1hp more. In 1950, a Model MG6 arrived with an 8hp two-cycle one-cylinder Drayton diesel. The

1950 Fowler-Marshall VF Crawler
Messers. A. and L. Carter had owned this VF crawler for about seven years when this photo was taken. For three of those years, it was in pieces. Then they got serious about finishing the restoration process. The tractor is a 1950 model. It has six forward speeds and two in reverse and weighs about 6 tons. It is quite a handful to control in tight places, such as loading on a trailer. Steering is by hand brakes for each track.

MG6 weighed about 1,400lb. Later, a much improved MG-40 was presented, which used a Sachs 10hp one-cylinder air-cooled diesel.

The Ramsomes had some interesting characteristics. The use of rubber track joints was pioneered on the MG series. They were also noted for the use of a centrifugal automatic clutch and a unique reversing mechanism using two crown wheels in the differential. They were steered by hand brakes.

1959 Ransomes MG6 Crawler

Here is a crawler that will plow for two days on a gallon of diesel fuel. Of course the plowing rate will be about an acre per day. Ransomes is an old-line British farm implement manufacturer. The first of these mini-crawlers came out in 1936. Through the end of production in 1966, more than 15,000 of various types were made. They were mostly used by nurserymen and market gardeners, but many were shipped to The Netherlands and Tanzania where they could be moved from field to field by small barges. The 1959 model shown is owned by P. Dolman of Burwell, Cambridgeshire.

Previous page
1956 Ransomes MG6
Although it may look like it is a gas turbine, power for this 1959 MG6 comes from a one-cylinder two-cycle air-cooled diesel made by Drayton. It produces 8hp. A variety of engines have been used to power the Ransomes mini-crawler. Some are gasoline (petrol), some are diesel.

1956 Ransomes MG6
P. Dolman's 10-year-old son, Ian, sits at the controls of this 1959 MG6 for size comparison. Features of the MG6 include rubber jointed tracks, a centrifugal clutch, differential brake steering, a hydraulic lift, and a three-forward, two-reverse transmission. Dolman carries the 1,400lb crawler in his VW van, pulling a caravan (camping trailer) besides.

Previous page
1947 Bristol 20
This rare crawler was made by the Bristol Automobile Company in 1947, in Bristol, England. It is powered by a 16hp Austin four-cylinder car engine. The Bristol is 3ft, 3in wide. This one is owned by Arthur Farnes of Hailsham, Sussex.

1947 Bristol 20
After World War II, the Bristol crawler was made for horticultural nurserymen and market gardeners. The Bristol used "Roadless" rubber-jointed tracks. The owner, Arthur Farnes of Hailsham, Sussex, is in the driver's seat. He has owned this machine for about four years. He found it in a scrapyard, about to be cut up. Features of the nifty 3,000lb Bristol include a three-speed transmission, hand clutches and foot brakes, three-point hitch, PTO, and electric start.

Chapter 12

Modern Farm Crawlers

Last fall on the top of Diamond Ridge, we came upon warning signs that logging was in progress along the forest road on which we were traveling. Suddenly the crisp cold of a late fall morning was pierced by the high speed whine of a diesel powered, rubber tired, articulating four wheel drive skidder bringing a turn of logs suspended by an integral arch. With a ridiculous little blade in front, headlight eyes, and churning tires mounted on steel arms, it looked like a giant praying mantis with a clutch of sticks to build its nest. The age of tracklaying tractors is nearing its end as inherent friction spells its doom. What a grand and glorious time it was when "cats" on endless tracks roamed the woods.
—James A. Young and Jerry D. Budy, *Endless Tracks in the Woods*

In the last few decades, many of the tasks that were once the job of the grand old tracklayers have been taken over by rubber-wheeled vehicles. Yet there are some areas that are still the province of the crawler, and likely to remain that way for the foreseeable future.

The most prominent of these is the crawler bulldozer. There seems to be no practical size limit to these monsters. Some, like the 770hp D11 Caterpillar, must be assembled on the job site; it's as large as a small house. The last of the Allis-Chalmers (before the Fiat-Allis merger of 1974), the HD-41, had a bare weight of over 101,000lb. It could be equipped with a 30ft blade.

Deere and International Harvester left the big end of the market to others (increasingly dominated by foreign marks). Deere's largest, the 850, registers 165hp.

1990 Caterpillar Challenger 65
Stanton Phelps of Rockton, Illinois, owns this Cat Challenger; Stanton's son Bob is at the controls. The Stantons farm 2,500 acres with the Challenger and several other big tractors. They like the Challenger because it causes less soil compaction. The Challenger 65 has a 636ci engine which produces 290hp. It has a ten-speed power shift transmission with two reverse speeds providing a road speed of nearly 20mph.

Caterpillar, Deere, and others have pioneered innovative control methods to make the crawler more productive. The John Deere 850, for example, has dual hydrostatic drives that proportion power to each track. Most of the larger Cat models now have differential steering after all these years. It's not the same as the

1993 Caterpillar D11N
Caterpillar's version of the irresistible force, the giant D11N, shown in Caterpillar's indoor demonstration arena. It is powered by a 770hp V-12 diesel. The occasion was a tour provided for the Antique Caterpillar Machinery Owner's Club in November 1993. Club members are shown examining the machine.

1990 Caterpillar Challenger 65

The most modern of the agricultural Caterpillars are the Challengers. These are the unique all-purpose farm tractors with the Mobil-trac track system. Mobil-trac includes a rubber track with eight pneumatically supported bogies on each side. The system provides superb ride comfort and allows speed (18mph), mobility, excellent flotation, and good traction. A state-of-the-art cab is standard equipment. It is, of course, heated and air conditioned. It is also pressurized to keep out dust and chemicals. This 1990 Challenger 65 is owned by Stanton Phelps of Rockton, Illinois. It weighs about 28,000lb, and is equipped with a two-way radio, cellular telephone, and a full electronic computerized instrument panel. Stanton has some fairly wet ground, which he would be unable to get into in the spring were it not for his Challenger.

old system pioneered by Cletrac, however, but a hydrostatic differential speed trimmer that divides power between the tracks according to the position of the steering controls. On many of the modern crawlers, steering can be done by feet or hands; some have only foot controls.

Have we come to the end of the road for farm crawlers? Has the articulated all-wheel-drive, sometimes with twelve tires, completely replaced the tracklayer?

"Not at all," says Case-International. The merged firm is currently working on an agricultural crawler running gear for its four-wheel-drive tractors.

"Not at all," says Caterpillar. Cat's current brochure shows six models designated "agricultural tractors." Two more models are in the works.

First, and most obvious, of the modern agricultural Caterpillars are the Challengers. These are the unique all-purpose farm tractors with the revolutionary Mobil-trac system. The Mobil-trac includes a rubber track with eight pneumatically supported bogies on each side. The system provides unexcelled ride comfort and allows high speed (18mph), mobility, and excellent flotation and traction. It combines the best of wheels and tracks. Challengers come in two sizes (the 65 and 75), but soon two more will be added (a 45 and an 85).

Challengers use hydrostatic differential steering controlled by a steering wheel so driving is much the same as a wheel tractor. During turns, power is proportionally applied to each rubber belt, or track, to enhance traction and to provide smooth even turns. A state-of-the-art cab is standard equipment. It is, of course, heated and air conditioned. It

is also pressurized to keep out dust and chemicals. The cab is rubber-mounted and has sound suppression features.

An electronic-display instrument panel is divided into three parts. The left side uses light-emitting diodes to warn of high transmission, steering, or hydraulic oil temperatures. There are also parking brake, low fuel, and alternator warning lights. The right panel shows tillage and application functions. Read-outs show ground speed, slippage, total acreage, acreage per hour, engine hours, and several other functions. A center panel shows oil pressure, coolant temperature, and engine rpm.

The Challengers come with PTOs and three-point hitches. The transmissions on the 65 and 75 models are ten-speed power-shift units. Details of the 45 and 85 models are not available at this writing. The engine of the 65 is a six-cylinder 638ci unit boasting of 271hp. The Model 75 is powered by a slightly smaller (629ci), but turbosupercharged and aftercooled six-cylinder engine rated at 325 gross horsepower. The Model 65 weighs about 31,000lb, while the Model 75 weighs about 33,000lb. Ground (foot-print) pressure is about 5.5psi for almost negligible soil compaction.

1980 John Deere Model 450E
This Model 450E John Deere was for sale at Joe Schloskey's Machinery Hill in Phillips, Wisconsin. Schloskey has rebuilt the machine to be "like new." The 450 is a 60hp machine.

The other four Caterpillar agricultural models are the SA (Special Application) versions of regular crawler models. These include the D3C SA, D4E Custom SA, D6D Custom SA, and the venerable D8L Custom SA.

1992 Case International QUADTRAC
The Case International QUADTRAC, exhibited at the 1992 Farm Progress Show, is a concept demonstrator not yet committed to production. It was designed to respond to farmer's concerns about soil compaction with increased tractor weights.

Appendix

Sources

Clubs and Newsletters

Newsletters providing a wealth of information and lore about individual brands of antique farm tractors and equipment have been on the scene for some time. More are springing up each year, so the following list is far from complete.

Antique Caterpillar Machinery Owner's
  Club
Marv Fery, President
10816 Monitor
McKee Road NE
Woodburn, OR 97071

Antique Power
Patrick Ertel
PO Box 838
Yellow Springs, OH 45387

Two-Cylinder Club (John Deere)
308 East 6th Avenue
Grundy Center, IA 50638

Green Magazine (John Deere)
R. & C. Hain
RR 1
Bee, NE 68314

I.H. Collectors (IHC)
RR2, Box 286
Winamac, IN 46996

M-M Corresponder (Minneapolis-
  Moline)
Roger Mohr
Rt 1, Box 153
Vail, IA 51465

9N-2N-8N Newsletter (Ford)
G.W. Rinaldi
154 Blackwood Lane
Stamford, CT 06903

Ford/Fordson Collectors Assn.
Jim Ferguson
645 Loveland-Miamiville Road
Loveland, OH 45140

Old Abe's News (Case)
David T. Erb
Rt 2, Box 2427
Vinton, OH 45686

Old Allis News (Allis Chalmers)
Nan Jones
10925 Love Road
Belleview, MI 49021

Oliver Collector's News
Dennis Gerszewski
Rt 1
Manvel, ND 58256-0044

Prairie Gold Rush (Minneapolis-Moline)
R. Baumgartner
Rt 1
Walnut, IL 61376

Red Power (IHC)
Daryl Miller
Box 277
Battle Creek, IA 51006

Wild Harvest (Massey-Harris-Ferguson)
Keith Oltrogge
1010 S Powell
Box 529
Denver, IA 50622

Books

The following books offer essential background on the crawler's origins and history, and about the tractors and equipment of the times. These make good reading and library additions for any tractor buff. Most are available from Motorbooks International Publishers & Wholesalers, PO Box 2, 729 Prospect Avenue, Osceola, Wisconsin 54020 USA, or by calling 1-800-826-6600.

The Agricultural Tractor 1855-1950, by R.B. Gray, Society of Agricultural Engineers; an outstanding and complete photo history of the origin and development of the tractor.

Allis-Chalmers Tractors, by C. H. Wendel and Andrew Morland, Motorbooks International; in Motorbooks' Farm Tractor Color History series, replete with photos of beautifully restored Allis tractors.

The Allis-Chalmers Story, by C. H. Wendel, Crestline Publishing. The complete history of the A-C line with lots of archive photos.

The American Farm Tractor, by Randy Leffingwell, Motorbooks International; a full-color hardback history of all the great American tractor makes.

Benjamin Holt & Caterpillar-Tracks and Combines, by Reynold M. Wik, American Society of Agricultural Engineers; a scholarly study on the life and genius of Ben Holt, one of the founders of Caterpillar.

The Caterpillar Story, published by Caterpillar. It details important history of the founders of Caterpillar and of how things got to be the way they are.

Caterpillar Tractors 1926-1959, written and published by Peter J. Longfoot; a model by model description of all the great Caterpillars.

The Development of American Agriculture, by Willard W. Cochrane, University of Minnesota Press; an analytical history.

Endless Tracks in the Woods, by James A. Young and Jerry D. Budy, Crestline Publishing; a complete, detailed and readable account of the history of the crawler tractor and its relationship to the logging industry.

Farmall Tractors, by Robert N. Pripps and Andrew Morland, Motorbooks International; IHC history and tractor details along with sparkling photography. One of Motorbooks' Farm Tractor Color History series books.

Farm Tractors 1926-1956, Randy Stephens, Editor, Intertec Publishing; a compilation of pages from *The Cooperative Tractor Catalog* and the *Red Tractor Book*.

Fordson, Farmall and Poppin' Johnny, by Robert C. Williams, University of Illinois Press; a history of the farm tractor and its impact on America.

Ford Tractors, by Robert N. Pripps and Andrew Morland, Motorbooks International; a full-color history of the Fordson, Ford-Ferguson, Ferguson and Ford tractors, covering the influence these historic tractors had on the state of the art of tractor design.

Ford and Fordson Tractors, by Michael Williams, Blandford Press; a history of Henry Ford and his tractors, especially concentrating on the Fordson.

Great Tractors, by Michael Williams and Andrew Morland, Blandford Press; some of the world's most classic tractors are described in words and pictures.

Harvest Triumphant, by Merrill Denison, WM. Collins Sons & Company LTD; the story of human achievement in the development of agricultural tools, especially that in Canada, and the rise to prominence of Massey-Harris-Ferguson (now known as the Verity Corporation). Rich in the romance of farm life in the last century and covering the early days of the Industrial Revolution.

Nebraska Tractor Tests Since 1920, by C. H. Wendel, Crestline Publishing; a synopsis of all the tractor tests since the beginning of the program.

150 Years of International Harvester, by C. H. Wendel, Crestline Publishing; a complete photo-documented product history of International Harvester.

150 Years of J. I. Case, by C. H. Wendel, Crestline Publishing; same as the above, but for Case.

Other Interesting Publications

For a directory of Engine and Threshing Shows, Stemgas Publishing Company issues an annual directory. Their address is:

PO Box 328

Lancaster, Pennsylvania 17603

The cost of the directory has been $5.00. It lists shows in virtually every area of the country. Stemgas also publishes *Gas Engine Magazine* and *Ironmen Album*, magazines for the enthusiast.

Index